STEP BY STEP
Woodcarving

STEP BY STEP
Woodcarving

ALAN AND GILL BRIDGEWATER

Bell & Hyman

Dedicated to the memory of
Leslie George Hill and George Babey.

Published in 1985 by
Bell & Hyman Limited, Denmark House,
37/39 Queen Elizabeth Street, London SE1 2QB

© Alan and Gill Bridgewater 1985

ISBN: 0 7135 2572 X

British Library Cataloguing in Publication Data
Bridgewater, Alan
   Step by step woodcarving.
   1. Wood-carving
   I. Title   II. Bridgewater, Gill
   736'.4   NK9704

Acknowledgements
We would like to thank all those people who helped
us with this book – a special thanks must go to Julian
and Glyn for being good boys, to Terence Donovan
for help with the photographs and to Barry Martin of
Henry Taylor Tools Limited for his help and
assistance.

Photograph acknowledgements
The Scandinavian Bible box (p. 12), French pedal
harp (p. 14), Japanese Netsuke mouse (p. 68), old
English trestle stool (p. 99) and the Grinling Gibbons
carving (p. 112) are reproduced by courtesy of the
trustees of the Victoria and Albert Museum, London;
the Polynesian paddle blade (p. 12) and American
north west coast Indian bird-shaped bowl (p. 82) are
reproduced by courtesy of the Horniman Museum,
London and the American rocking horse (p. 13),
Pennsylvanian German plate rack (p. 87) and New
England Bible box (p. 93) are reproduced by courtesy
of the American Museum in Britain. All other
photographs belong to the authors' collection.

Designed by Colin Lewis
Typeset by August Filmsetting, Haydock, St. Helens
Printed in Great Britain by
The Bath Press, Avon

Contents

Introduction

I sometimes take one of my woodcarvings, close my eyes and then run my finger tips over its form and textures – it's a wonderful feeling. To follow the flowing and softly undulating lines of the wood grain; to remember the hours spent crisply cutting sweet smelling wood and then to open my eyes and to know that the carving has been worked and created with my own two hands – these are beautiful, unique experiences that should not be missed. The ambitions of this book involve sharing with you all the finger tingling pleasures of woodcarving.

In the short section at the beginning of the book all the basic woodcarving techniques are briefly described. These are followed up with eighteen progressive, very detailed step by step, illustrated projects and a chapter at the end provides information on tools, timbers and technical terms. Each project opens with an introduction that places it in a geographical, historical and cultural context. Then with a great many working drawings and photographs the book gently takes you through the various exciting stages of designing, buying wood, considering the tools and materials, using the tools, sawing, carving, finishing and so on.

Don't misunderstand me, this isn't one of those books where the projects are so boringly easy that they aren't worth doing anyway. Every project will, in one way or another, present you with a good solid challenge and each project relates to, is inspired by, or has its roots in, a specific wood carving tradition or technique. There are such items to carve as love tokens, Art Deco frames, American decoy ducks, foliate masks, Japanese netsuke and Black Forest figures. I have tried to achieve a balance between ethnic, tribal, folk and western sophisticated wood carving and I hope that by tackling each of the projects in turn the beginner will gradually increase his knowledge, expertise and confidence, and along the way create wooden articles that are unique, personal and beautiful.

Basic Woodcarving Techniques

A note on sharpening your tools

One of the secrets of woodcarving is knowing how to keep your tools keen and razor sharp. You must have a flat, coarse, bench stone; a fine textured oil-stone; a selection of wedge shaped stones and slips; a strop leather; oil and crocus powder. The overall theory is straight forward and simple enough – damaged or really dull tools are angled and bevelled on the coarse stone. The bevelled edge is refined and honed on the oil-stone and the burrs are removed with the strop, oil and crocus powder.

Chisels
Grinding Hold the chisel at an angle of about 15° to the horizontal. Then slowly rub it backwards and forwards across the coarse stone – continue until the bevel is even, clean and level.

Honing Dribble a little light oil on the fine stone, hold the chisel at 15° and rub the blade backwards and forwards across the stone until the bevel is shiny. Now raise the handle slightly and continue rubbing until the blade edge is keen and sharp.

Stropping Dress the strop leather with oil and crocus powder, place it on the bench and draw the honed chisel blade across the leather until all the burrs have been removed.

Gouges
Grinding Hold the gouge blade at 15° to the grindstone and gently rub the gouge from side to side across the stone. But this time, as you rub, rock the gouge so that the whole of the bevel comes into contact with the stone. Continue like this until the whole curve of the bevel is angled, even and well set-up.

Honing Oil the fine stone, hold the gouge at 15° and then repeat the side to side rocking and rubbing. Try to get the bevel to a shiny finish, then raise the handle of the tool very slightly and continue with the rocking and rubbing until the edge is keen.

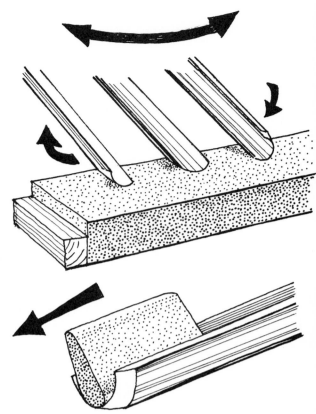

Sharpening gouges – the bevel is rubbed and rolled across the oil stone until the cutting edge is keen and razor sharp and the shaped slip is used to polish the inner bevel.

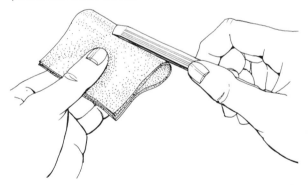

Once the outer bevel has been worked on the oil stone and the inner bevel has been polished with a stone slip, the burrs are rubbed off with a folded leather strop.

Stropping Finally take the oiled and crocus powdered leather and rub off all the burrs, as with the chisel sharpening.

Note: I always think that there are as many ways of sharpening tools as there are carvers – spend an hour or two trying out different tool angles and holds, and then go for the method that suits you best.

Whittling

Although 'whittle' originally comes from the middle English word thwitel and the Anglo Saxon thwitan, meaning to cut and pare with a small, belt-slung knife, I think that now it is generally accepted that 'to whittle' has come to mean any small, not too serious carvings, that have been made and worked in the American folk tradition. In the modern, American sense of the word, whittled carvings are folk made, spontaneous carved items like paper knives, small figures, trick chains, animals, caricature figures and the like.

I think of whittling as being the simplest and most direct of all the wood carving techniques. All you need is a good sharp knife and a lump of wood, and you are off. So if you are looking for a simple direct wood craft, one that can be worked with the minimum of equipment and put down or taken up at any time, then whittling could be for you. If you are interested, start by looking for a good sharp, carbon steel knife that is comfortable to hold. I use a small pre-war bone handled penknife and also a couple of Henry Taylor chip knives that I have ground down and shaped. You might use a vegetable knife, a sheath knife, an old cut-throat razor or anything else that takes your fancy. Don't heed the advertiser's blurb about shiny bladed, all-purpose wonder knives. All you need is a sharp knife that you can happily push and pare – it doesn't matter how ugly it is.

Whittlers traditionally use just about any wood that comes to hand, such as white Pine, Lime, Holly, Box or Yew. As long as it is reasonably straight grained and free from dead knots, split ends and the like, then it's suitable. It has been said that there are as many methods and techniques of whittling as there are whittlers, but of course there are specific cuts and knife holds – pare, push, stab, stop-cuts and so on. However, in general terms, whittling is nothing more than holding the wood to be carved in one hand and pushing, working and manoeuvring the knife with the other. Or, as a crusty old whittler once advised, 'you need a friendly knife, a friendly wood and the rest is up to you.'

Chip carving

Chip carving is a traditional folk and ethnic technique of surface decorating smooth faces of wooden objects. Patterns and geometrical grids are drawn out over the surface of the wood and then the designs are worked by chipping out little triangular pockets. By

Whittling with a traditional Canadian crooked knife, a beautifully made, very efficient tool.

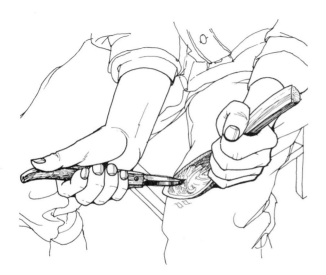

When chip carving the wood is held securely with a bench holdfast and the triangular pockets are worked with vertical and sloping cuts.

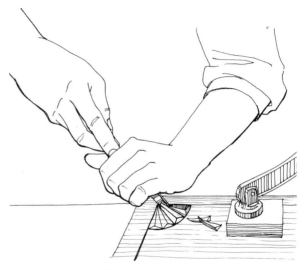

repeating vertical and sloping cuts and varying the arrangement and composition of the pockets, it is possible to triangulate all manner of smooth, curved or undulating surfaces with the most startling carved designs and motifs. The beauty of chip carving is that, by its very nature, it can be either extended in a free way and used as a total textural finish, or it can be restricted and used for regular, well defined border, edge and band decorations.

The tools needed for chip carving are no problem – a skew pointed knife, a sharpening stone and a G-clamp and you can consider yourself well equipped. Chip carving is best worked on a smooth close-grained, knot-free wood like Lime, Canary or satin Walnut. A piece of prepared wood, or better still a made-up item like a cigar box, is chosen; designs are drawn up and then the pattern is chipped out. Chip carving is simple and easy to do – in fact it's a perfect carving technique for beginners.

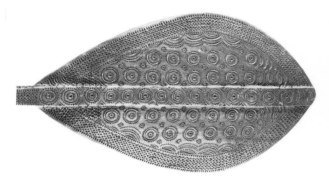

Polynesian paddle blade knife incised and chip carved. Worked in a smooth hard grained wood.

Incised carving

Incised carving is equally simple and straight forward. Designs are drawn out on the wood and then the lines of the design are cut and worked with either a knife or V-tool. With incised work there is no modelling in the sense that the designs are carved at different levels – the V-section incised lines are in themselves the sum total of the design.

Eighteenth-century Scandinavian Bible box worked in a primitive folk style. The design has been relief carved and modelled.

Low and high relief carving

Low and high relief carving can be thought of as a logical extension of incised work. Once the designs have been set out and incised, the carving is then taken one step further by being set-in, wasted or grounded. The carving technique is simple enough – the carver takes a gouge or some such scoop-tool and then cuts and lowers, little by little, all the wood that is considered to be outside the design. Once the ground has been cut away and lowered the

Relief carving – once the unwanted ground wood has been lowered, the raised design can be detailed and modelled.

high relief plateaux of the design are modelled and carved so that they have depth, shape and form. There are a great many variations on the basic technique, with designs being stylized, realistically modelled, deeply undercut, pierced and so on. But in general terms low and high relief carvings are all plank worked pictures in the sense that they are attached to a background, namely furniture and architecture, and carved so that they can only be viewed from the front.

As for tools, I think that most relief carving can be managed and worked with about twelve small section edge tools – a straight chisel, skew chisel, three or four straight gouges, a veining tool, a bent gouge, spoon bit gouge, a spoon bit chisel and a straight V-tool. Although relief carving is best worked on hard woods, my advice is to try any wood that comes to hand such as Oak, Walnut, Lime, Canary, Pine, Teak. As long as the wood is reasonably straight grained and free from knots, splits and warps, then it's workable.

The term carving in the round is used to describe a carving that can be viewed from most angles – usually taken to mean free standing sculptures.

Carving in the round

'In the round' is a term used to describe carvings that are more or less free standing and can be viewed from most angles – usually sculptural carvings like animals, figures,

Early nineteenth-century American folk made rocking horse which has been glued, pegged, built up, carved and painted.

plants and abstracts. For example, church bench-end poppets, Grinling Gibbons cherubs and modern creative sculptures could all be described as being in the round. This type of carving can be worked with twelve edge tools (as can relief carving) but you would also need a good selection of general wood working tools like a hand drill, coping saw, straight saw, surforms, rifflers and of course a work bench and vice. My advice to beginners is to start in a small way with the minimum of tools and clutter, and then to carefully build up your collection of tools when you are more experienced and able to see your needs more clearly.

The wood a carver might use would be anything from an apple tree blown down in a storm to reclaimed demolition roof timber. Try any wood that comes your way, and if it cuts cleanly and is free from knots, splits and rusty nails, then it's suitable.

Built-up work

The term 'built-up' is used generally to describe just about any carving that, because of size, depth or style, requires that separate pieces of wood be laminated, glued, nailed, screwed or pegged together. For example, a large free-standing carved figure might have a glued on addition for an outstretched arm or a small intricate carving might be made up of several different wood types, colours and textures. Although this type of carving needs no special tools or materials, it does require that the carver has a broad understanding of mechanical stresses, glues and resins, and also has a feeling for piece-meal, put together composition.

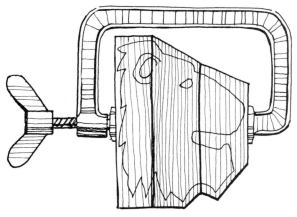

The term 'built-up' describes any carving that is made up from separate pieces of wood. In this instance three pieces of wood are glued and clamped.

Eighteenth-century French pedal harp. See how the carving has been relief worked, pierced, modelled, built-up and worked in the round. If you look closely at the leaves and acorns you can see where the laminations are cracking apart.

Seventeenth-century English Limewood carving. Although most of this carving has been cut from a single piece of wood some of the flowers are in fact built-up, glued and pinned additions.

Whittling

Paper-knife

The form and design of this knife were inspired by ethnic African and Oceanic woodcarving. Traditional carvings from these areas are alike and unique in that when they were made the designs and forms related only to local needs, myths and methods of working – there were very few outside influences. Although the shapes of the carvings and the styles of the designs and patterns are exciting and full of movement, meaning and symbolism, they are, generally speaking, technically basic and simple in detail. The designs, patterns and motifs tend to be chip carved and incised, with plenty of zig-zags, flat relief geometrical shapes and coloured mastic inlays.

Traditional African societies were settled and organized with a stable fuedal system within which tribal groups were able to develop craft skills such as weaving, painting and woodcarving. This last was one of the most important crafts because of its many practical uses. The tools employed were very simple – the adze, the curved knife and the bow drill. Woodcarving skills, techniques and traditions were jealously protected and only passed on from father to son or master to pupil. In this way designs, patterns, motifs and ideas changed and evolved slowly, always referring to the immediate past. Shapes and designs always related directly to the availability of suitable woods, the tools used and the function of the carving. Domestic bowls and

Inspirational carving of a selection of African and Oceanic chip carved and incised decoration.

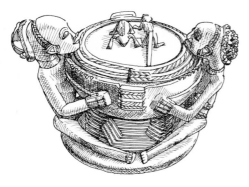

Inspirational carving of nineteenth-century African tribal woodcarved pot with figure supports and incised and chip carved decoration.

dishes were usually made by local village woodworkers, while the more prestigious ritual and ceremonial relief-carved bowls, pots, stools and staffs were worked by professional master carvers.

All carved patterns and motifs were useful in the sense that they were spiritually and religiously significant – African woodcarvers wouldn't have understood the function or meaning of abstract decoration. A bowl or dish might be decorated and supported by all manner of naturalistic figures and chip-carved patterns, but it would be considered that each and every carved mark or motif contributed to the spiritual well-being of the bowl owner or user.

Oceania includes New Zealand, Melanesia, Micronesia and Polynesia and all these areas have, as far as we are concerned, similar woodworking traditions. The highly organized tribal and cultural activities of Oceanic societies included making war, hunting, religious and spiritual ceremonies. For all of these activities it was necessary to have the correct accoutrements – masks, bowls, plates, weapons and canoes, all of which needed to be

Inspirational carving of a design taken from a nineteenth-century Maori feather box. Note how the pattern grid has been stylized and chip carved.

carved and decorated with significant motifs and symbols. Working with adzes and knives made of stone, bone, shell and later, iron, the carvers worked naturalistic, symbolistic and chip carved designs on just about everything. Woodcarved bowls and dishes were functional in that they held water and had spouts, handles and the like, but at the same time it was necessary that they be pierced and patterned with complex, swirling, chip carved spirit motifs. For example, a New Zealand Maori carved door lintel not only functioned as a structural support, it also protected the entrance to the building with its stylized bird men figures and surface chip carved decoration.

Method
Simple whittling using chip carving and incised line

Working time
3–8 hours

Tools and materials
For this project you are going to need an easy to work, straight-grained, knot-free, light-weight wood – a wood that will hold a hard-edged, knife-cut design. You could try Holly, Willow, Lime, Kauri Pine (a favourite with New Zealand carvers), or even a bit of driftwood or found green-wood. Whatever wood you decide to go for, check up that it cuts cleanly and that it is free from dead knots, splits, shakes and soft bark edges. If you do decide to use a piece of found wayside green wood, strip off the bark. Make sure that there aren't too many branch spurs and choose a length that is relatively straight grained.

For tools and equipment you will need an axe; mallet; drawknife or spokeshave; a couple of good knives (say a clasp knife) and a chip carving knife together with bits and pieces from around the workshop such as pencils, sketch paper, a measure and the use of a vice and holdfast.

If you look at the illustrated carved and decorated paper-knife you will see that it is about $8\frac{1}{2}$in long, $1\frac{3}{4}$in wide at the handle and about $\frac{3}{4}$in thick. However, if you have in mind something a little smaller or fancier, then adjust the working drawing to suit. But remember that you need a good broad area for the chip carving and incised line decoration.

Setting out and carving the form
Take up your bit of wood and look at it thoroughly all over. Is it about the right size for your hand? Is the wood a good colour? Are there any pulpy knots? And so on. When you are sure that your piece of wood is right for the project you can then start setting-out and transfering the design.

If you have prepared wood, all well and good, but if like me you are going to start with a rough lump, then you need to take the mallet and axe and split the wood to size. Aim to make a billet of wood that measures about 9in long, $1\frac{3}{4}$in–2in wide and $\frac{1}{2}$in–1in thick, and then mark it up with a central working line, as illustrated.

Now clamp one end of the billet in the vice and set to work with one or other of the shaping tools – the drawknife or the spokeshave. Carve and work the billet until it is flat-oval in section, full and rounded at one end

Chip carved knife (made by the author). Carved out of smooth-grained, knot-free Lime wood. Note the smooth uncomplicated form and the small delicate decoration.

and swiftly pointed at the other. I must say that this part of the project isn't quite as easy as it looks, because as the wood begins to take shape, so it becomes more and more difficult to hold. I tried making a couple of wooden V pipe jaws for the vice and I also tried muffling the wood with old felt and clamping it to the bench, but in the end I settled for holding the wood in one hand and shaping it up with a knife held in the other.

When you consider that the carved form is just about complete, pick it up and pass it from hand to hand feeling out its qualities and faults. Could the wood be smoother? Does the handle fit snug in your hand? And so on. Finally rub the wood down with a bit of fine grade sandpaper and then bring it to a silky finish with beeswax and a fluff-free cloth.

Drawing up the grid

If you have a good look at my working drawing, you will see that the chip-carved and incised bands of pattern cover about 3in of the knife handle. If you feel that this is too much or not enough now is your chance to adjust the design to suit. Take up the carved knife form, pivot it between the work surface and your finger tips and then with a steady hand mark in the design grid, as illustrated.

My design is based on an $\frac{1}{8}$in, $\frac{1}{4}$in, $\frac{1}{2}$in grid – there is a $\frac{1}{4}$in band of pattern, a clear space of

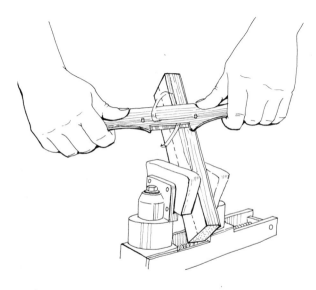

Put the billet of wood in the vice and with the spokeshave work it until it is flat-oval in section.

Bring the roughed-out billet to completion with a knife.

Working drawing – the grid scale is four squares to 1in. Note the direction of the grain.

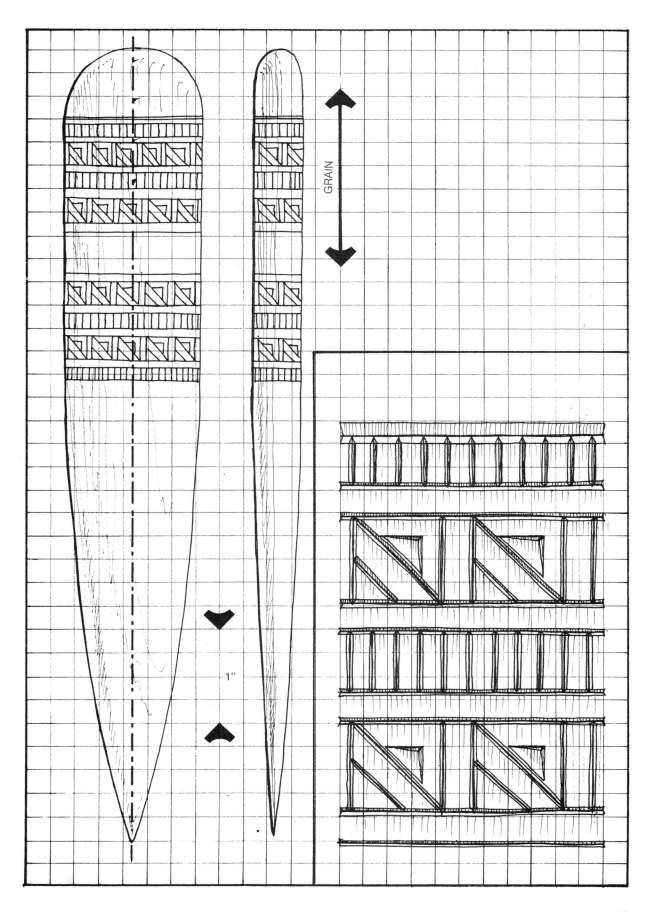

GRAIN

1"

Pivot the carved form between the work surface and finger tips and draw in the design guide-lines.

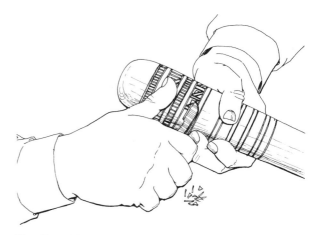

Finally, with two vertical cuts and a single sloping cut remove the little triangular pockets of wood.

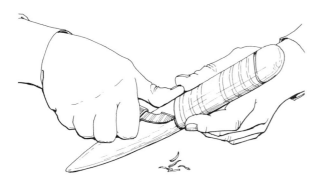

Cut V-section trenches that follow the drawn lines.

about $\frac{1}{8}$in, a $\frac{1}{2}$in band of pattern, another clear $\frac{1}{8}$in band and then the sequence is repeated. You can either draw in the grid lines by eye or you can work out a little marking gauge with, say, a pencil and ruler or a pencil and wooden blocks.

Chip carving and incised lines

Once the design grid has been drawn in, you can start the chip carving and incising. There are a great many ways of actually working the wood and holding the knife. For example, you might clamp the wood to the work surface and, holding the knife like a dagger in the right hand, guide it with the finger tips of the other hand; or, like me, you might prefer to hold the wood in one hand, cradle it in your lap and then hold and guide the knife with the other hand. However, it isn't really the actual manner of working that's important – it's the results that count.

Incising is simple enough. The object is to cut a V-section trench that follows the lines of the design. Two cuts are made, one at an angle into the other, so that a thin sliver of wood curls away. You work the whole design in this manner, all the while cutting little V-trenches. It's all relatively straight forward, the only tricky part being the cutting of any V-trenches that follow the grain. You do have to be in total control of your knife and you must watch out that the blade doesn't run into the grain and split the wood. Cutting out the little chip carved triangles is just as simple – two cuts are made so that they meet each other at about 90° and you then slide your blade down into the cut angle and cleanly lift out the little triangular nick of wood. Always support and guide the knife blade with both thumbs. Finally brush away the chips of wood, tidy up any ragged edges and the job is done.

Hints, tips and afterthoughts

The secret of chip carving is having a well set out design grid – take a lot of trouble setting this out. A good sharp knife is also a must – I use a short blade, single edge, purpose made chip carving knife. With chip carving and incised lines, remember that there is a lot of thumb work. As the cutting blade is drawn towards you across the wood always support, control, guide and manoeuvre it by the lever and pivot action of both thumbs.

Love-token puzzle chain

Whittled love-tokens are, by their very nature, one-off items that were carved and given in token of love. Picture if you will a lonely shepherd lad sitting out the winter in an isolated cottage and dreaming of his sweetheart and wife-to-be back home. No books, radio or television, so what better way of 'whittling away the hours' than by making an almost impossibly complicated present for his beloved. And so it was all over Europe, Britain and colonial America, with lonely lovestricken lads whittling and carving symbolic tokens of love. Intricate puzzle chains carved out of a single piece of wood; plump twined hearts carved with dates and initials; whittled love-spoons; corset busks decorated with incised hearts and flowers, and so on. In many ways wood carved love-tokens can be thought of as valentines – decorative, non-functional, symbolic expressions of love. Traditionally, love-tokens were knife whittled by amateurs with no special tools, woods or techniques. Just a good sharp knife, a knot-free white wood and the desire and the determination to do better than the next man.

Method
Knife whittling in the round

Working time
10–12 hours

Whittled love-token (made by the author). Lime wood, knife carved and incised. When choosing your wood make sure that it is totally knot-free.

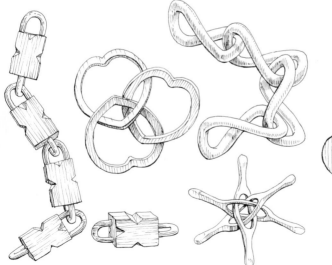

Inspirational carvings of puzzle chains and love-tokens which come in a great many shapes, types and sizes.

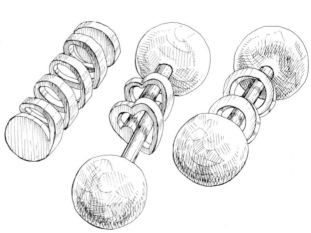

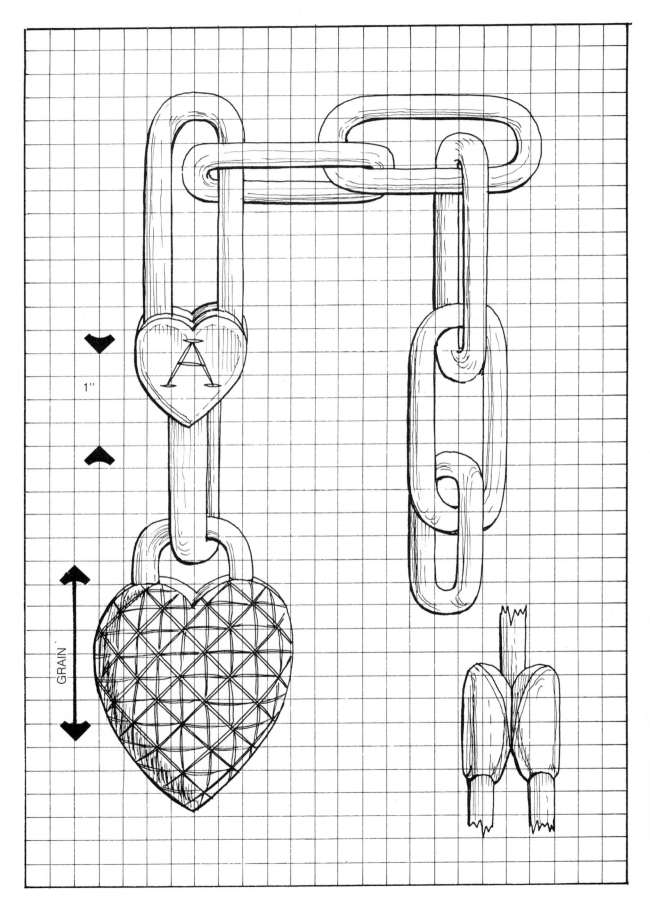

1"

GRAIN

Tools and materials

For this project you need a razor-sharp penknife and a nice length of prepared, smooth-grained, knot-free wood. Look around for an off-cut of Lime, Holly or some such easily worked white wood that is approximately 2in wide, 1in thick and 12in long. You will also need some work-out paper, a measure, pencil and plastercine.

Before you put pencil to paper or knife to wood, consider the project well and take a good, long look at the working and inspirational drawings. Try and decide in your mind's eye just how you want the design to be organized. Are you going for the heart and chain as photographed? Or would you prefer to try your hand at a more complex piece, say the three-heart shaped links? Or maybe the balls and links? Whatever you decide, when you have a clear picture of the carving, set it out on paper and then make a full size mock-up with the plastercine.

Setting out the design

Once you have looked thoroughly over your piece of wood and checked that it is free from stains, end splits, warps, knots and grain twists, you can then set out the design, as illustrated in the working drawings.

With the ruler and pencil divide the 1in wood thickness into three equal parts. Draw two parallel lines round the wood thickness, sketch in the shape of the two hearts and finally set out the position of the chain links. When you are sure that all is correct, shade in the areas that have to be cut away, and then clearly label the wood *top, side, link 1, link 2* and so on. If at this stage you can't quite see how the links are to be cut and worked, make a plastercine model of the block of wood and have a dry run.

First cuts

Start by cutting away all the unwanted wood, that is, the two corner pieces at the bottom of

Working drawing – the grid scale has four squares to 1in. Note the direction of the grain and the detail of the 'A' heart.

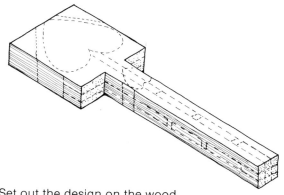

Set out the design on the wood.

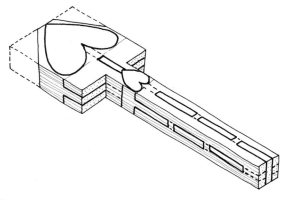

Cut away the two corners of unwanted wood at the bottom of the heart.

Cut away the strips of wood that run up each corner of the chain until the stem is cross shaped in section.

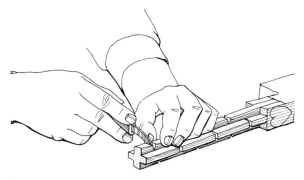

Once you have established the cross shaped section cut out the stop-cuts between the links.

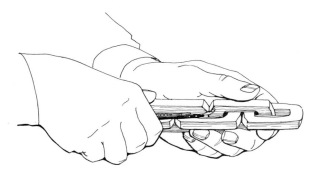

Deepen your cuts until the eyes of the chain begin to take shape.

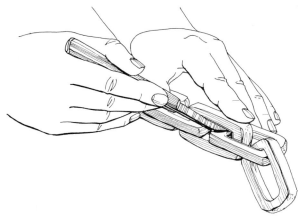

Cut away all the unwanted wood in and around the links and finally, with great care, cut through the bridges. This part of the project is tricky.

Detail of the heart shapes.

the heart and the two strips that run up each side of the chain. Carefully whittle away the shaded areas of the chain so that you are left

with a long stem of wood that is cross shaped in section.

Now for the tricky bit – re-establish with a pencil, the order, length and position of the links and then whittle out the stop-cuts between the links, as illustrated. The long stem of wood should now be notched at intervals so that the position and length of the links is clearly set-out. Next, with caution, deepen the stop-cuts until your knife begins to pierce the wood at the central cross and finally, the outside lines of the links need to be whittled, curved and brought to a good finish. This done, take the pencil and shade in the central eyes of the chain links.

Piercing the links

Take the knife, select two touching links and gradually work and carve the wood until you manage to pierce the eye of the link that holds them together. Now for the most difficult part of the project. Gently cut away all the unwanted material in and around each of the links until they are only held together by a slender bridge of wood. Now stop awhile, re-sharpen your knife and assess the situation. With extreme care, nibble away with the knife point at all four sides of the bridges until the links separate. You will find that once the first link has been cut free, all the others are comparatively easy and you will wonder why your first steps were so hesitant.

Finishing

When you come to carving the heart shape at the end of the chain look at the working drawings and you will see how the heart is, in fact, no more than a variation on the basic link theme. With this in mind, continue carving and whittling as before, but this time cut-in the wood at the end of the last link so that it pierces the wood at the top of the heart.

Once the bridge of wood that joins the last link to the heart has been cut away the rest is straight forward. Trim up all the areas of short grain at the end of each link and then go over the whole carving giving it a texture, pattern, initials, a tooled finish or whatever else takes your fancy.

Hints, tips and afterthoughts

It's a good idea before you tackle this project to have a trial run with a simple three-link chain. If your piece of wood is hard work and cuts up roughly, try sharpening the knife – if this fails, get another piece of wood.

If by chance in the final stages of the project you split a link, (I did), don't despair and kick the carving round the workshop. Glue the break immediately, wait twenty four hours and then get back to work.

The slender bridges of wood that hold the links together are difficult to work because not only are they inaccessible, but also the links at that point are short-grained, so work with care and maybe use a fine-point craft knife.

Inspirational carving. The actual size of this figure is 2½in, it's carved in Box wood and painted. I picked it up at a sale and I think it is about 100 years old and German.

American folk figure

When the settlers left their European homelands to build new lives in the American wilderness, they lived at first in turf huts and tents. But these temporary shelters were soon replaced by more comfortable cabins and homesteads. Naturally enough, the new Americans wanted decorations, furniture and household items that reminded them of the old country. As they couldn't afford imported goods they had to improvise – most of the settlers had their roots in small rural communities in England, Sweden, Norway and Central Europe, so their arts, crafts and designs tended to be simple, direct, naïve village-made echoes of back home. Gradually an American style of crafts such as woodwork and weaving, developed which we now describe as being American folk, pioneer American, colonial American, or homespun.

This folk style is characterized by direct, basic, whittle-carved ornaments, whittle-decorated furniture and knife worked items of kitchen ware. When a pioneer housewife wanted a bit of decorative carving for the best

room, a wooden toy for the children, a cake mould, a pastry wheel or a weathervane for the barn roof she would go and see the local whittler-woodworker or perhaps wait for a visit from one of the travelling woodworkers. These itinerant pedlars used to move around the countryside calling on farms and villages.

One such pedlar was a Pennsylvanian German called Wilhelm Schimmel. He travelled around with his horse and buggy, whittling toy ark animals, little jointed dolls for the children, and eagle ornaments for their parents. For a small fee and maybe a bed and board, Schimmel would also carve, whittle and make items to order. In my mind's eye I see Schimmel sitting in the shade of a barn with simple tools – a knife, saw and drill. No doubt a small group of mothers and children would soon gather round to gossip and watch him work. I imagine a housewife describing some ornament her mother had back home, and Schimmel desperately trying to please her by working her hazy description into an ornament or toy. Schimmel would always be on the lookout for interesting pieces of wood – he would perhaps see a bird or figure in a piece of branch-spur Pine or Juniper root and then quickly whittle and carve to a swift bold finish.

Whittled figure – a traditional piece made out of Pine wood and painted.

Whittling, in the tradition of the American pioneer and travelling man, needs to be bold and folksy with plenty of knife marks and angular shapes – not rough, not shoddy, not beautiful, just swift, direct and economical.

Method
Whittling in the round

Working time
2–3 hours

Tools and materials
For this project it's not so easy to say just what wood you should be using, because after all,

Inspirational carvings. If you are looking for ideas, look through comics and magazines and try to find figures that are chunky and tight.

whittling is a carving technique that spontaneously uses any found wood that comes to hand. However, in general terms you need a bit of wood about 6in–7in long, 2in wide and 2in thick as in the working drawing. Use wood that is straight grained, free from knots, splits and bark – maybe a bit of Box, Lime, Holly or even a piece of Yew.

Whittling tools are also something of a problem because whittlers tend to use almost anything that take their fancy such as old dinner knives, bits of broken hacksaw blades, razor blades or old kitchen knives. I use two Henry Taylor chip carving knives which are beautiful and I also sometimes grind a piece of spring-steel to shape to make a particular knife for a particular job. I suggest that you start by buying a couple of knives and then buy or make more knives when you feel the need.

Setting-out the design
Take a good look at the working drawings and see how I have concentrated on the main planes and forms. There are no fine details or fussy areas, just direct and swift knife-cuts. Take your piece of wood and with some sketch paper, tracing paper and a pencil, draw in the various views and elevations. Notice how the proportions are worked – the head is about 2in long which is about one third of the total height. Don't aim to whittle a life-like figure, just look at the main features – the nose, the heaviness of the chin and the weight and bend of the shoulders, and then work a caricature that captures the essentials. When you feel that you understand how the figure ought to be carved, pencil in the main lines and block-in the areas of wood that have to be chopped out.

First cuts
Take up the wood and the knife and start by making stop-cuts around the lines that indicate the bottom of the shawl, headscarf and forehead; the angle between the chin and chest, and the bottom of the dress. Cut straight down into the grain to a depth of about $\frac{1}{8}$in–$\frac{1}{4}$in. Now hold the wood so that the

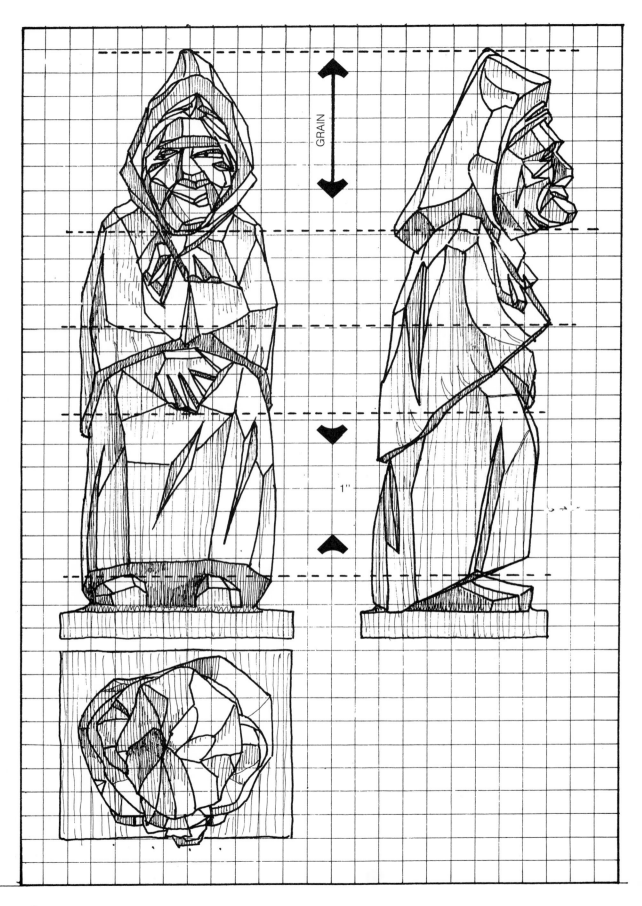

GRAIN

1"

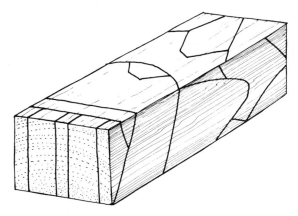

Pencil in the main lines of the design and block in the areas of wood that are to be chopped out.

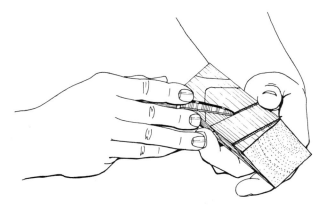

Make stop-cuts around the shawl, headscarf and forehead cutting into a depth of $\frac{1}{8}-\frac{1}{4}$in.

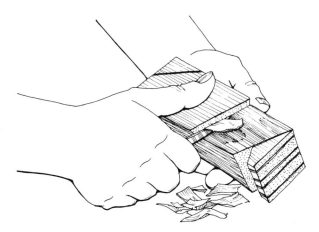

Pare, carve and shape the wood, continuing to cut into the stop-cuts.

Working drawing – the grid scale is four squares to 1in. Note the direction of the grain.

head end is nearest to you, take the knife and chop at an angle into the stop-cut at the bottom of the shawl. Work round the figure so that there is a clear step at the shawl bottom. Continue in this way over the whole of the figure by paring and carving into the stop-cut lines. Once the steps are clearly worked you should be able to see the figure coming out of the wood.

Whittling the face
Look closely at the profile, as illustrated, and you will see that the face is in fact made up of a series of stepped cuts. Hold the figure so that it is face uppermost and feet nearest you and holding the knife as if you are going to pare an apple start whittling the features. Cut sharply down into the wood from the edge of the headscarf to the forehead; cut in from the forehead to the eye line; cut in from the point of the nose to the eye line and so on down the face. Keep making big bold cuts that establish the heavy, stepped profile and finally, still holding the figure in the same position, chop out the shapes of the forehead, cheeks and heavy chin.

Finishing
When the features have been whittled out go swiftly over the rest of the carving, chopping out the shape of the crossed hands, shoes, central hair parting, point of the head and so on. Don't scrape or sandpaper – the knife

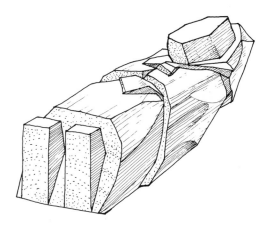

Once you have established the main form, start to round up the figure with single direct knife cuts.

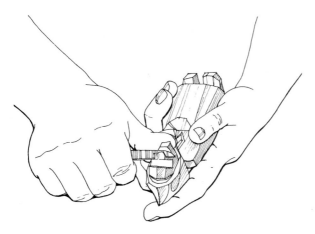

Knife carve the face with a series of stepped cuts. Don't try for fussy detail but keep the features rugged and heavy.

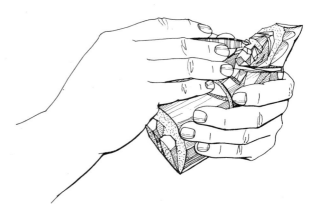

Finally, with a very sharp knife cut out the mouth and eye slits.

should be so razor sharp that it leaves the wood crisp and clean. Finally, with some water colour washes and a fine brush, paint in the main blocks – say, black for the dress, a brown and yellow plaid, a blue/white head-scarf, flesh brown for the face and hands and finish up by dotting in the eyes with black spots.

Hints, tips and afterthoughts
When whittling, most cuts are made with a simple thumb-push paring action of the knife. It the wood cuts raggedly, then either it is damp or the knife needs sharpening.

When you come to carving the face, keep the cuts tight and not too deep, and watch out when you come to the short-grain nose and chin.

If, by chance, you should split off the nose or chin or, indeed, anything else, don't despair – just improvise and change the figure accordingly.

Relief and Chip
Carving

Jack-in-the-Green

Primitive man saw the growth, death and renewal of trees and believed that in some way his own life was controlled by the spirits of the greenwoods – trees and human sacrifice, Jupiter and sacred Oaks, druids and sacred groves. It has been suggested that these are all expressions of the belief that man's life depends on, and is linked to, the spirits that live in trees. In the dark ages when Christianity was being grafted onto the old religion, churches were more often than not sited near sacred trees and built of 'spirit' Oaks.

Over the centuries, as ideas advanced, the tree spirits were given three dimensional form and represented by woodcarved foliate figures and masks. In medieval times the carvers who worked our churches, drew their inspiration from things around them and from traditions handed down from father to son. These carvers would have taken part in ritualized tree-worship celebrations when villagers dressed up as green men, the green man, Jack-in-the-green, Hairy men of the woods and Lord of the trees. These simple rural craftsmen worked all their personal and traditional experiences into church carving – foliate masks spewing leaves; Jack-in-the-Green faces with tendrils snaking out of the eyes and mouths, and grotesque faces crowned with greenery all of which represented tree spirits. It's an uncomfortable experience to catch sight of a contorted and twisted foliate face peering out from a dark corner of a country church and to know that it has been hiding there week after week, year after year, century after century and that it is a direct link with a pagan past of magic, fertility and tree worship.

Method
Relief carving

Working time
16–24 hours

Tools and materials
Before you start out on this project it would be a good idea to visit a few early West Country

Jack-in-the-Green foliate mask (made by the author). Relief carved and undercut Lime wood, stained and painted and finally waxed.

churches or maybe take a trip to one of our old cathedrals, such as Wells or Lincoln. Look at the bench ends and the misericords and see how the primitive carvings have been considered and worked. Search around in dark corners (how about underneath the seats?), and use a pair of binoculars to look at high up carvings, and you will be sure to spot a foliate face. These masks or faces come in a great many shapes, forms and sizes, but generally speaking they are characterized by having gaping, gargoyle mouths, vine tendrils and foliage sprouting out of the eyes, mouth or ears, and have an overall expression of leering unhinged malevolence.

When you have absorbed the feel of these carvings and think you have some understanding of how they were conceived you can start work. Look around for a suitable slab of 1in thick wood, something that measures about 13in × 13in would be perfect. You could use an easy to carve wood like Lime and then darken it to suit the character of the carving, or maybe you would prefer to use a massive slab of Oak or Walnut and work with the knots and grain twists. The choice is yours. For tools

Inspirational carving of a Jack-in-the-Green from Christchurch Priory, Hampshire.

A Jack-in-the-Green face on a bench-end at Brent Knoll Church, Somerset, England.

A foliate face from a sixteenth-century English cupboard.

you need a bow or coping saw, a rasp or spokeshave, a medium V-section tool, a shallow-curve straight gouge, a couple of spoon bit gouges and other tools from around the workshop such as a measure, compass, scrap paper, tracing paper, pencil, sandpaper and rifflers.

Setting out the design

When you have had a good look at our inspirational drawings, walked around a few old churches and generally gathered together a collection of character face pictures, foliage, magazine clips and details of eyes, ears and mouths, then you are ready.

Start by taking your slab of wood and the compass, set out a good generous circle, mark the centre and draw in a centre line. Then cut your wood to shape with a bow saw and rasp.

Inspirational carving of an early sixteenth-century Jack-in-the-Green misericord in St Mary's Church Newark, Nottinghamshire, England.

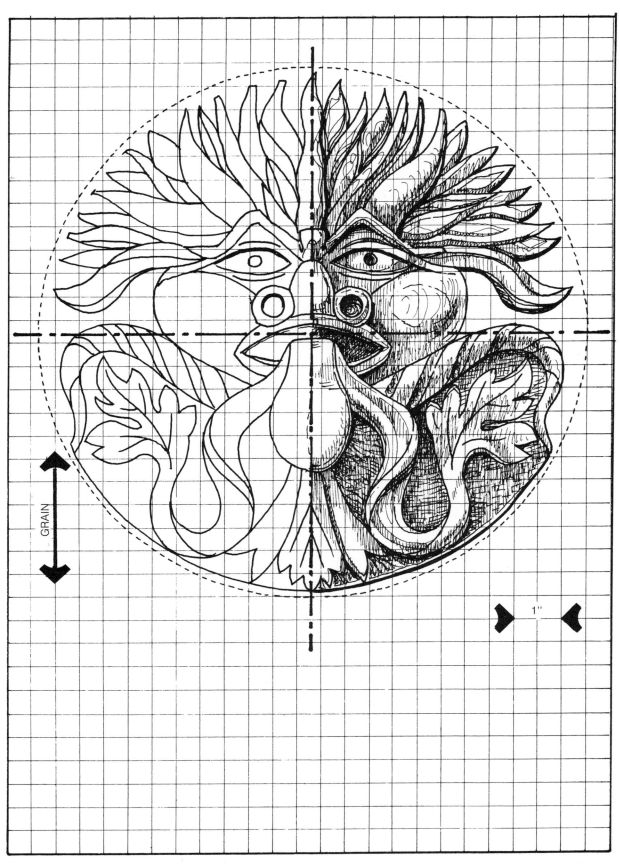

GRAIN

1"

Working drawing. The grid scale is two squares to 1in. Note the direction of the grain and the overall symmetrical circle based design.

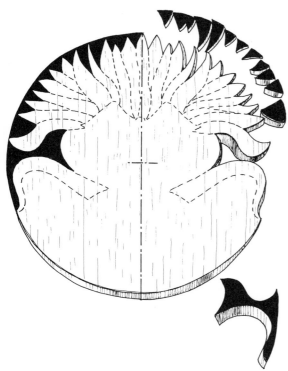

Draw out the design and cut away the unwanted wood.

Once you have established the main lines of the design cut them in with a V-tool. Note how the wood is secured with a G-clamp.

Once you have cut-in the lines of the design with the V-tool you can either set-in with a straight chisel and then gouge away the unwanted ground, or you can remove the ground and then set-in. In this instance you do have to be careful not to split off fragile areas, so leave the initial setting-in and model the details with a straight gouge and spoon bit.

Take your sketch paper, tracing paper and a soft pencil and work up the main lines of the Jack-in-the-Green design. Go for a broad, wide eyed, open mouthed, high cheeked face and decide whether or not you want the face to be symmetrical. Now you can pencil press transfer the lines of the design onto the wood. When the design has been transferred, set about making all the pencil lines clear and strong and indicate just how you want the wood to be worked whether it should be cut away, lowered, pierced or some other technique.

First cuts

Put the slab of wood in the vice or clamp it to the work bench and then take the bow saw or coping saw and start to cut away the unwanted areas. If you look at the photograph of my Jack-in-the-Green you will see that I have cut into the disc of wood at the hair line and removed the wood to emphasize the bulge of the cheeks. Follow and manoeuvre the saw blade around the form, but watch out that you don't split the wood at the fragile, side, short-grain areas.

Cutting-in

Once the slab of wood has been roughed out, clamp it flat to the workbench; look again at all your inspirational material and then arrange the tools comfortably to hand. Take the V-section tool and cut in the main lines of the face, the shape of the mouth, the set of the eyes, the nostrils, tongue and so on. You will be working both with and across the grain, so be on your guard and be ready to check your tool if you feel it is biting too deep or sliding into the grain. When you come to the hair, deepen the V-cuts, but be careful that you don't twist the tool and split the grain. If you are using Lime there should be no problem –

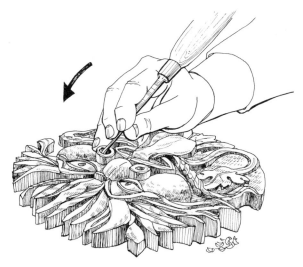

Scoop out the nostrils with a small spoon bit gouge, working with a gentle hooking action.

Detail. Note the depth of the ground and the undercuts under the tongue.

Finally, clean up the carving with a riffler.

you just hold the tool in one hand and push and manoeuvre it with the other. If you have chosen to use a hard character wood like Oak, then you will need to drive the tool with the mallet.

Setting-in and modelling

With the straight gouge and the spoon bit gouges, deepen the V-cuts around the nostrils and the mouth and then start to carve the cheeks using the V-cuts as stop-cuts. As you carve the broad curve of the cheeks, slice out the dips around the nose and mouth and generally lower the wood, so that the nose will stand out and the cheeks begin to look full and rounded. Aim to emphasize the bulge of the lower eyelids, the shape of the mouth and the flare of the nostrils. Try to slide the gouges across, or at an angle to, the grain and try to keep all the cut forms fluid and alive. Carve the full bulge of the cheeks, cut away the rough saw-cut edges and always check on the thickness of wood that you have left. Once you have established the overall shape and form of the nose you can start to carve the nostrils. Either carve into a pre-drilled guide-hole or gouge out the hole in total. Whichever method you choose, use a small spoonbit gouge and be sure that you don't lever your tool on the side rim of the nostril and split the wood.

Continue working the whole of the carving in this manner – extending and deepening the initial V-cuts, lowering the unwanted wood and modelling the form. As the Jack-in-the-Green face starts to come alive you will find that you have to continually modify the design to suit the spirit of the wood. For example, if you feel that the swirl of the grain suggests a new feature, or an interesting knot has design potential, be flexible and prepared to rework the carving to suit the changing conditions. From time to time, as you are carving, take a mirror and maybe twist your mouth, poke out your tongue or spread your lips – see how your features move and fit together, and then work what you have seen into your design. The leaves and tendrils need to be carved just like the more formal relief carved projects the design is cut-in with a V-tool, the unwanted ground is lowered – and the leaves and other decorations are modelled. One of the joys of this project is that you can use the carving to express your own flights of fancy – there are very few design rules or restrictions.

Finishing and colouring
Take the sandpaper and the rifflers, rub down the rounded forms of the cheeks and tongue and then clean up all the creases and corners. If you have chosen to use a light coloured wood like Lime, tint it with some water colour washes in red, brown, orange and black. Darken the creases and pick out the proud wood with yellow and orange highlights. Finally, when the paint is dry, break up the colours with a scrap of sandpaper and give the whole carving a good polishing with a brown tinted furniture wax.

Hints, tips and afterthoughts
This project is best worked with a character wood like Oak or Walnut. You could use a piece of wayside wood you have found or even carve a tree stump in situ.

When you come to carving the foliage, it's a good idea to have leaves, twigs, ivy or other decoration close at hand to use for reference.

If you have to colour and darken a light wood, don't use spirit dyes because they tend to smother and kill the grain. It is much better to use tints, tones and highlights of thin water colour washes.

Art Deco Mirror Surround

Art Deco was never a single art and craft movement but was a coming together of art and industry. After the first world war it was gradually realized that mass produced items need not be ugly because they were factory-made but they could be positively designed so that they became objects of beauty. For the first time in history artists and designers sat

down and designed functional items such as electric fires, kettles, chairs, fabric and pottery. Although the designers idealistically set out to 'produce forms that were honest expressions of production and function' they couldn't help but be influenced and inspired by the period in which they lived.

'Those tremendous times between the wars, 1919–1938, . . . it was a time for Bright Young People – women's hair was at its shortest – hats were bell shaped and cloche – lips were cupids bows and Jazz and the Charleston were all the rage.'

The designers, sculptors and carvers, inspired by the new and the modern – cars, speed, aeroplanes, trains, radio, cinema, archaeological finds in Egypt and central America, Russian Ballet and Cubism – evolved a decorated art style that we now call Art Deco. The carving of the period is characterized by flat

Inspirational carving, of a design carved on a cabinet by Paul Follot for the 1925 Paris Exhibition.

bas-reliefs that have been described as bold, massive and crude – Greek and Egyptian women in brightly coloured zig-zag costumes and huge square-jawed, cubist and revolutionary inspired figures. Generally speaking, Art Deco sculptures and carvings were commissioned, not by wealthy individuals who wanted soft, subtle, romantic imagery, but by multi-nationals and public corporations who wanted prestigious, heraldic expressions of power, success, monetarism and modernism.

Method
Bas-relief

Working time
8–10 hours

Inspirational designs of Art Deco figure motifs, New York 1931. Note the zig-zag drapes.

Inspirational design taken from a painting by Metzinger titled *Girl with a Bird*.

Materials and tools
The Art Deco style is a difficult one to catch because it was really a flickering reflection of the quick-changing twenties and thirties scene. However, after a great many rough sketches and work-outs I decided to design and carve an Art Deco motif pastiche. I gathered up the most obvious Art Deco clichés – for instance, Egyptian figures, zig-zags and sunbursts, and enclosed them in a radio speaker form. The design isn't meant to be subtle, brilliant or artistic – it's just a piece of pleasuresome whimsy that is fun to carve.

I decided to work this project in Lime wood because primarily I needed a light coloured wood that could be tinted with water colours and I didn't want to be over concerned with difficult wood grain and texture. For this project you need a piece of Lime about 11in wide, 13in high and 1in thick – see the working drawings. I used only the most basic tools – a coping saw, a small V-tool, a shallow-curve straight gouge, a straight chisel, a chip-carving knife and, of course, a pencil, compass, tracing paper, measure, rasp, sandpaper and water colours.

Before you start, take a good look at the working drawings and photographs. I have designed the frame to take a 9in × 6in mirror tile (the mirror just clips on to the back of the frame) but if you want something bigger or narrower change the scale to suit.

Setting out the design
Start by changing and adjusting the design as you think fit and then draw up a grid. Work the design to scale on a sheet of tracing paper and when you are happy and sure that the overall design fits your scheme of things pencil press transfer the lines of the design through to the working side of your wood.
Note: Make sure the wood grain runs from top to bottom.

Working drawing and detail – the grid scale is two squares to 1in. Note the direction of the grain and the Art Deco imagery.

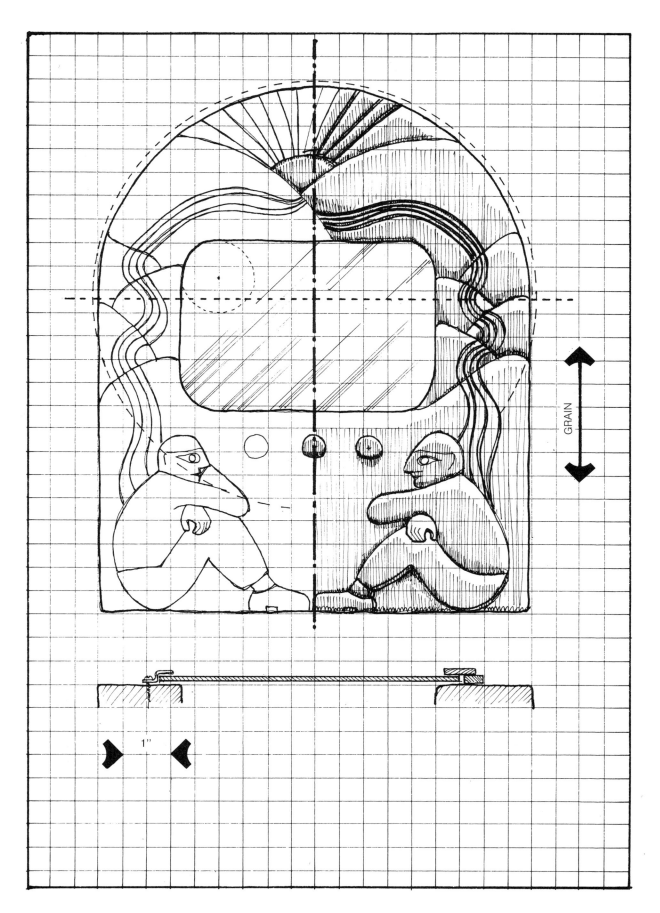

GRAIN

1"

Once you have transferred the design, pencil over the main lines, block in the areas that have to be chopped out and generally label and organize the wood. At this stage I usually make little notes on the wood to be carved, like *leave this bit, cut deeply here, leave to last* and so on.

When you are ready to start carving, pin all your working drawings around the workshop, brush down the work bench and arrange all your tools so that they are comfortably at hand.

First cuts

Secure the wood in the vice or G-clamp so that it hangs over the edge of the work surface and then with the hand drill, coping saw and rasp, rough-out the basic, round-topped, pierced window form. This is quite a small carving that is going to be looked at every time someone peers in the mirror, so double check that the window is nicely worked and the top curve is smooth, symmetrical and well finished. Work the curve from side to top with a rasp or spokeshave, as illustrated, and then you won't chop into the end grain and split the wood. Finally take the rasp and the sandpaper and trim and rub-down all the tight curves and edges.

The basic motifs

Clamp the roughed-out form to the work bench and look over it — if the design is in any way blurred or unclear, take a soft B pencil and strengthen the lines. Now take the chip carving knife or the V-tool, as you prefer, and cut-in the design. When you make the V-cuts around the two figures watch out that you don't cut too close or too deep — $\frac{1}{8}$in away from the waste side of the design and $\frac{3}{8}$in deep would be fine.

I actually made the V-cuts with the chip carving knife rather in the manner of the Japanese wood block cutters holding the knife like a dagger in my right hand and pulling it around the design guiding the blade with the fingers of my left hand. It all sounds complicated but don't worry if it's not the way you

Art Deco mirror surround (made by the author). Relief carved in Lime wood and painted.

work, since the actual manner of working isn't really important, it's the results that count. The object is to cut a V-shaped trench in all the lines of the design — a cut that keeps on the waste side of the design and slants slightly away from the design. This method of carving produces shapes and motifs that are strong and broad based. It also means that when you cut away the waste ground there is less chance of damaging the fine short grain areas.

Setting-in and lowering the waste ground

The lines of the design should now be established so you can start to work on the two seated figures. Take the shallow-curve straight gouge in both hands and gradually lower the waste ground — push and thrust with one hand and guide and manoeuvre with the other. Don't even try to work a level, regular depth ground. Remove most of the wood to a depth of $\frac{1}{8}$in and then cut-in deeply along the form describing V-cuts and the edge of the design. When you work with Lime you can certainly take liberties like cutting in almost any direction and more or less ignoring the grain, but for a really smooth pleasant crisp cut, I suggest that you work the gouge at a sharp angle to the grain. If you look at the illustrations you will see that of all the motifs and areas, it is only the two figures and the radio knobs that stand out in high relief – bear this in mind when you are lowering the waste wood.

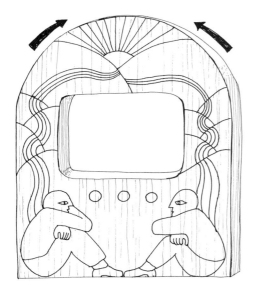

With the drill, coping saw and rasp, cut out the basic shape. Note the direction of cut for the rasp.

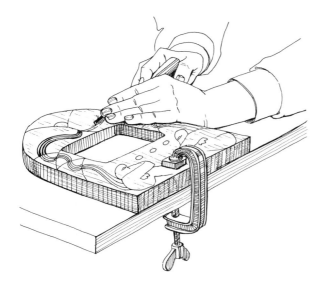

With the wood G-clamped to the work bench, take the V-tool and cut-in the drawn design.

With the shallow curve gouge, lower the unwanted ground wood around the two figures. Note, if you haven't got G-clamps you can use bench stops or blocks of wood screwed to the work surface.

Modelling the forms

Brush down your work surface, re-arrange the tools and then stand back from your work and be very critical. Are the figures and motifs well set-in and established? Is the waste ground low enough? When you are reasonably sure that all is well and you have a good picture in your mind's eye of how the carving is going to look you can start to model the various forms. **Note:** If you have any doubts or problems as regards form, it is always a good idea to make a few sketches and maybe do some workouts with some plastercine or clay.

Take the knife or gouge and gently cut away and round off the sharp corners and edges of the high relief figures – don't try for heavily undercut and modelled realism, it is much better to keep the forms tight and stylized. Feel your way around the separate elements of the design – trousers, hands, heads, always trimming, shaping, cutting and rounding to establish and rework the forms.

Look at your working drawings and the photograph and you will see that the illusion of roundness and three dimensions has been achieved by cutting and sloping the planes so that the various design elements appear to be layered one on top of another. For example, the hills rise out of the wood like waves, and there are sharp peaks and deep troughs. Once you are happy with the modelling of the hills you can take a sharp knife, or the V-tool, and cut-in the stream – try and keep all the curves rounded and fluid.

The sunburst

Once you have cut-in the position of the sun with the knife or V-tool, you can begin to model the rays. Each ray must rise wedge-like out of the sun, grow in height and width, and then stop just short of the top curve of the

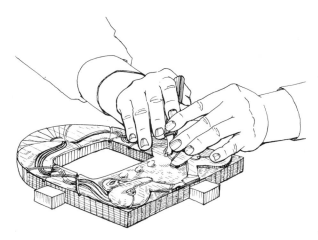

When the ground has been lowered take the knife, and round and model the relief forms. Keep the overall design tight and stylized.

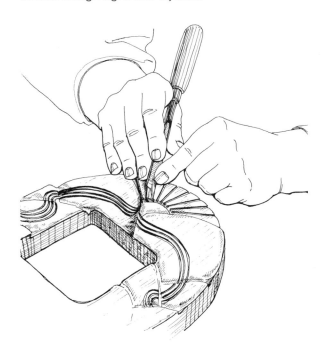

Use a knife or V-tool to cut in the rays of the sunburst. Watch out for changes in grain direction and try to keep the rays sharp and straight edged.

frame. Take up the knife or the straight chisel and work from the top curve down into the sun, continually slicing at an angle to the grain of the wood. Each ray sits on a radius struck off from the sun and needs to be worked straight and sharp edged.

Finishing

Once you have carved all the motifs and are reasonably pleased with the overall design you can give the whole carving a quick tooled finish. Tidy up and edge here, cut a sharper angle there and generally go over the whole carving making sure the design is crisply worked and pulled together. Finally, brush out all the little angles and corners and make sure the whole project is free from dust and shavings.

Painting

When I designed this frame I had a particular room setting in mind and wanted the frame to be delicately tinted with water colours. Maybe you would prefer the wood to be left natural, waxed or sprayed – give it some thought! If you decide to go for the water colours, don't put them on in one thick coat. It is better to mix up several thin washes and build up the colour density little by little. When the paint is dry take a piece of fine grade sandpaper and go

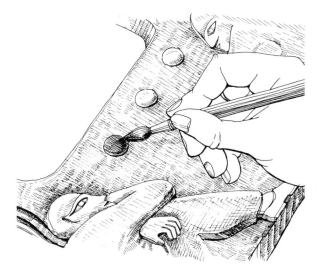

Paint the finished carving with thin water colour washes.

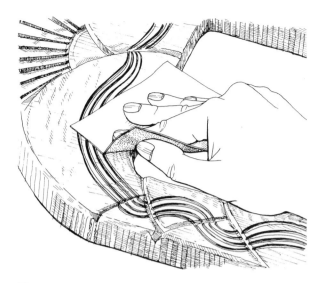

Finally, when the paint is dry break up the colours with a piece of fine sandpaper.

over the whole carving. Break the colours slightly to achieve a worn look, dust down, clip on the mirror tile and the job is done.

Hints, tips and afterthoughts

For me, this project was a quick, fun to do, one-off. It had to be Art Deco in character, it had to be coloured and it had to be a project that I could start and finish in a few hours. However, if you like the idea but want a project with more scope, you could go for a more exciting wood such as Oak or Walnut.

There's no need to carve the backs of frames or the underneath of chairs or boxes – just take a carving to an honest, direct and efficient finish.

Decorative panel

Of all the European decorative wood carving techniques, I think that chip carving is the oldest, the most basic, the most widely used and the most attractive. Paul Hasluck in his book *Traditional Wood Carving* published in 1911, says of chip carving, 'It belongs to the childhood of the world because it forms such a large part of the ornamental art of savage, or semi-savage, peoples, . . . it was introduced to the British Isles by the Scandinavians.'

Inspirational design of a traditional chip carved design with central roundel.

No one knows when, where or by whom chip carving was originated – but it is a most beautiful technique that has always been used the world over. Next time you are looking around a folk museum, stop awhile, search out the treen and some of the smaller pieces of kitchen hearth furniture, and you will be sure to find prime examples of chip carving – rose roundels on old English chests; chip decorated beds; boards and kitchen ware from Scandinavia; chip carved Celtic and Norse chairs and stools. Traditional European folk, rural or peasant, chip carved designs are characterized

Inspirational designs of motifs taken from English chests.

important element in the design is nearly always the triangular nick. These nicks, sometimes called pockets or three-cuts, are worked into overall designs and patterns by means of carefully organized, triangulated geometrical grids and repetition of the basic cut. These pockets are worked by three cuts – two vertical and one sloping, the finished design being either the pockets themselves or the areas of high relief wood between the pockets.

If you are a beginner to wood carving and you are looking for a gentle lead into the use of basic tools, wood types, cutting difficult grains and so on, chip carving is to be recommended.

Method
Chip carving with some incised work

Working time
6–7 hours

Tools and materials
Before you set out on this project, bear in mind that chip carving is best managed and worked on small areas of prepared, smooth, close-grained, knot-free wood such as Lime,

Nineteenth-century European chip carved panel carved from Lime wood.

by having sharp-edged triangular cuts that are worked within circles and geometrical grids – small carved objects, surface patterned with crosses, circles and zig zags with the spaces in-between filled with triangular chip cut and nicked designs. Most of the items made in the last hundred years or so were produced for the tourist trade, with small village or cottage industries making picture frames, letter racks, book ends and trays to name but a few. All are well made, skilfully carved and beautifully chip decorated with patterns, names, dates, crests and designs.

If you look closely at traditional European chip carvings you will see that the most

44

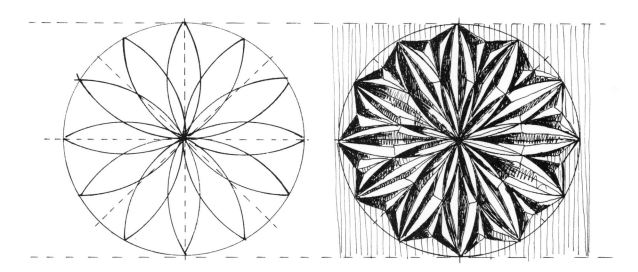

Inspirational designs of three ideas with compass worked guide-lines. See how even the most complicated design is still based on the three cut triangular pocket.

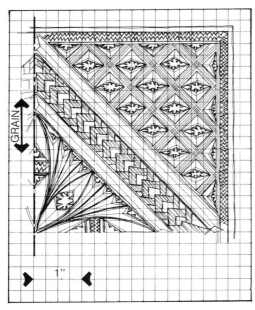

Working drawing – the grid scale is four squares to 1in.

Canary wood or satin Walnut. I chose to make a simple, decorative 8in × 9in Lime wood panel, but of course if you like the idea of chip carving but you're not so keen on the panel, then there is no reason at all why you shouldn't chip carve decorate something else. How about an existing table top, a stool seat, a tray or a picture frame? You only need to make sure that the chosen wood is smooth grained and workable. For tools you will need a small V-section parting or veiner tool, a really sharp knife (I use a couple of Henry Taylor chip carving knives), a fine blade saw and a compass, measure, square, pencils, tracing paper and rough work-out paper.

Setting out the design

Take your piece of prepared Lime wood, check it over for knots, warps and splits and then place it fair and square on the work surface. With the pencil, compass and ruler, establish the centre of the panel and draw in the diamond grid, as illustrated. With this project there is a lot of measuring and compass work, so take it a step at a time always following our working drawings and checking and re-checking measurements.

Set out the $\frac{1}{4}$in panel edge borders, zig zag borders, small diamond motifs, inner border,

deep V-section trench and finally the large compass worked central motifs. Look carefully at all the illustrations and working drawings and see how the large central motif is based on a single large circle and a series of compass-drawn half-circles and arcs. When you have modified, adjusted and drawn out the design, shade in the areas that are to be chip carved.

First cuts

Clamp the panel to the work bench, take up the small V-section tool and very gently set-in the main border lines that run around the

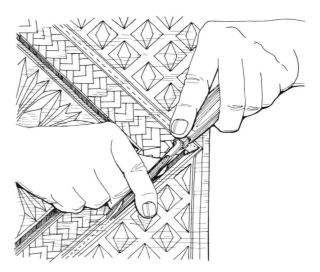

With a V-tool cut in the main lines of the drawn design.

Detail

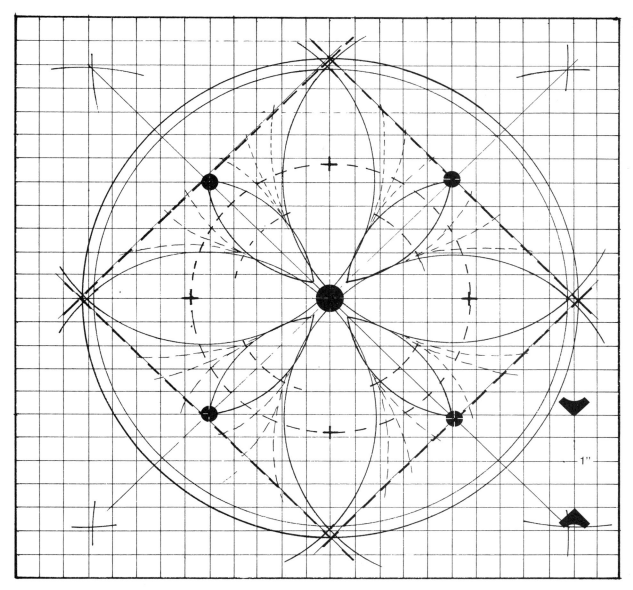

Working drawing – the grid scale is four squares to 1in. The central motif is compass drawn, quartered and arced – note the various centre points.

outside edge of the panel the lines that subdivide the small diamond motifs and the wide border that describes the main central diamond. The V-tool needs to be used with great care and a feather-light touch – just skim it over the wood and remove the finest of slivers.

The basic chip-cut

If you look at the illustrations you will see that all the chip carved designs, patterns and motifs are based on triangular pockets. Some of these are complicated by additional nicks

and others are long and curved, but they all relate to the simple three-cut technique.

Take your razor-sharp knife and hold it at the centre of one of the triangular pockets so that the blade is directed towards one of the three angles. Press the knife into the wood to a depth of $\frac{1}{8}$–$\frac{1}{4}$in and then draw it out towards the angle. Continue in this way cutting into the wood three times with every triangular pocket. Once the pockets have been set-in with three cuts you can work the design, pocket at a time, cutting away the wood that lies between any two cuts. The result of the three-cut technique (two centre to angle downward cuts and the single angled cut), is a little depression that looks like an upsidedown pyramid. It is the various combinations of these pyramids that make the total design. Of course, some chip cuts are more complicated than others in that the wood has to be left, curved or nicked, but basically they are all worked in a similar manner.

The central motif

If you look at the illustrated large central boat-shaped motifs you will see that although they are complicated by having curved sides, nicks

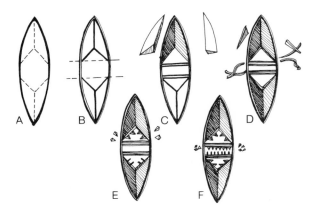

Cutting a double triangle pocket – **A**. Draw out the motif and the position of the cuts. **B**. Make cuts into the wood from the triangle centres to the angles. **C**. Cut at an angle into the three-cuts and remove the pocket of wood. **D**. Cut the incised central details with a V-tool. **E**. and **F**. Finally knife nick the central relief area.

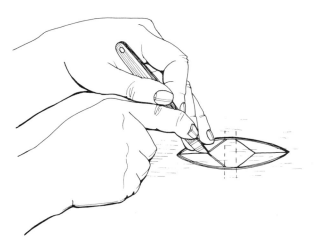

Cut straight down into the wood at the centre of the triangle and draw the blade out towards the angle.

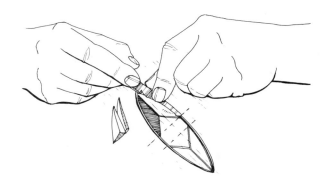

Make a sloping cut into the three initial cuts and remove the triangular nick of wood.

and relief areas, they are really no more than two triangular chip cuts worked back to back. Make three downward, centre to angle cuts at each end of the boat shapes and then with care, slide the knife at an angle down from the curved sides of the pocket into the wood, as illustrated. The sides of the triangle should now come away as neat slivers and you should be left with one section left in high relief. Do this twice with each boat motif to make the characteristic lozenge shape.

I do think that it all sounds incredibly complicated but it really is straight forward. However, if you are at all worried about spoiling a nice piece of wood or your best table top, have a trial run on a piece of scrap wood. Remember – each chip cut is made up of three downward cuts with the wood in-between the cuts being either removed or left in high relief.

The central motif border

If you look at the border around the central diamond the broad band of wood between the two deep V-trenches – you will see that rather than being worked with chip carving, it has been surface decorated with a delicate lattice of V-cut incised lines. The method is simple enough – the design is drawn, corrected and adjusted and the lines of the design are very gently skimmed off with the small V-tool. Finally, the texture within the border is achieved by close, V-tool, cross hatching.

Hints, tips and afterthoughts

Chip carving needs to be well drawn up and

set out and the secret of success is a well considered basic design, razor sharp knives and a smooth, close-grained wood. Certain areas, for example the long lozenge central pockets, might have to be deepened in stages, but nevertheless the overall method of working remains as described.

With chip carving it is vital that the wood cuts cleanly, so make sure you keep your tools keen edged.

When you have finished carving, brush out the chip cuts with a dry brush and wax the wood.

Adam and Eve picture frame

There is a style and type of early European wood carving that I think of as being 'primi-

Inspirational design of a detail from a twelfth-century Italian pillar.

tive'. For example, there are tenth-century Scandinavian church carvings that show curious figures and mythical beasts; ancient almost undatable thrones in our churches that are carved with inexplicable scenes and figures and church bench-ends that are so old they hark back to pre-Christian times. I don't group these carvings by reason of dates or location, but by the fact that they are all naïve, lively, figurative, almost tribal renderings of folklore fables, myths and Bible stories.

Although there are many such primitive carvings all over western and northern Europe, there are two that have particularly caught my imgination. One is a massive relief carving on a stave church at Urnes, Norway that illustrates the myth of Yggdrasill, the tree of heaven and earth, and the great serpent Nithoggr; and the other is quite a humble Saxon throne in St Mary's Church, Newark that illustrates the story of Adam and Eve. These two carvings are, no doubt, separated by hundreds of years, but for me they are closely linked by the fact that they were almost certainly conceived by simple, illiterate carvers who were using their skills and imagination to interpret colourful bardic accounts. You only have to run your fingers over these carvings and look closely at the beautiful naïve way the figures, motifs and symbols are grouped to know that they were created by inspired artist-carvers who with child-like directness were merely trying to make good pictures. Although these primitive carvers would have been commissioned and given size and material guide-lines, they would not have been restricted by transient notions of taste and good design. They listened to the bardic stories and then in a free and direct manner translated what they had heard into beautiful, bold, uninhibited wood carved pictures.

Method
Deep relief carving

Working time
8–10 hours

49

Inspirational design of a detail from a chair back, St Mary's Church, Newark.

Adam and Eve Frame (made by the author). Lime wood, gouge worked and wax polished.

Tools and materials

For this project you need to forget all your pre-conceived ideas of good and bad taste and work with what I can only describe as a child-like directness. Go straight into the carving. Don't get involved with style, figure proportions and the like just form a picture in your mind's eye of how you want the carving to look and then start work. If you are a beginner who just wants to have a go, then so much the better, this project is for you.

I decided to use Lime wood and work the Adam and Eve design into a mirror or picture frame. But, of course, there is no reason why you shouldn't use a slab of Oak or a piece of wayside wood you have found to carve a picture plaque, a table top or a house board.

You will need a generous slab of wood – a piece 13in wide, 15in high and at least 1in thick will be perfect. With this project don't worry too much about knots and grain twists as these can be used and built into your design. However, do avoid wood that looks as though it is split, excessively warped or has any loose dead knots.

For tools, you need a straight gouge, curved gouge, skew chisel, mallet, rasp, V-tool, small spoon bit gouge, knife, coping saw, hand drill and a G-clamp and pencil.

Setting out the design

Take the slab of wood, check it for splits and warps and then place it squarely on the work surface. Work out exactly how you want the overall design to fit and sketch the main lines, motifs and figures directly onto the wood. Do you want full figures? Are you going for a symmetrical design? Decide just how you want your design to work and block it in with a soft pencil. At this stage, don't bother to draw in any fine details – it is better to establish the big bold shapes and cross hatch areas that need to be cut away.

First cuts

Put the wood in the vice, or clamp it to the bench, and then with the drill, coping saw and rasp, rough out the basic shape and cut away the central window. Once this is done, take the rasp and rub down all the sharp sawn edges and re-work the pencilled guide-lines.

Setting-in the design

Clamp the slab of roughed out wood to the work bench and with the mallet and skew chisel, chop into the pencil lines of the design. Now take the V-tool and cut-in the coils of the

Draw out the design and cross hatch the areas of wood that need to be cut away.

GRAIN

1"

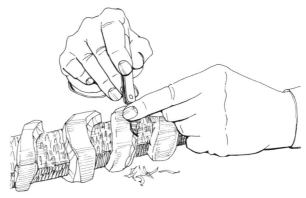

Once you have roughed out the basic frame, re-establish the lines of the design and lower areas of ground between the coils of the snake, in the branches and either side of the figures.

snake, the twined branches of the tree and the main lines of Eve's hair. If you look closely at the drawings and illustrations you will see that the tree between the coils of the snake has to be lowered. Take the spoon bit gouge and working across the grain, scoop out the wood between the snake coils lowering it by about $\frac{5}{8}$in. Don't try to lower the wood in one great wood-ripping scoop, carve it out layer by layer. Continue to work the whole carving in this way, establishing the lines of the design with the V-tool and lowering the unwanted ground with the spoon bit or curved gouge.

Modelling the forms

Once you have established the various levels of the design, take the straight gouge and knife and model the figures and forms. Cut away the sharp sawn edges, round off the coils of the snake and begin to work the shape of Eve's shoulders. Don't try for anatomical accuracy, just go for simple doll-like shapes. At this point pause to decide on textures, details and main features. If you look at my carving, as illustrated, you will see that I have drawn

Working drawing – the grid scale is one square to 1in. Note the direction of the grain.

When you have lowered the wood in and around the coils of the snake, take the knife and start to round and model the various forms.

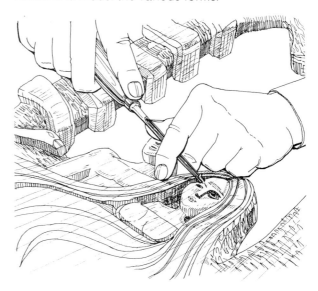

With the V-tool, establish the lines of the hair, the eyes and so on, all the time being careful that you don't split the wood or cut too deeply into the grain.

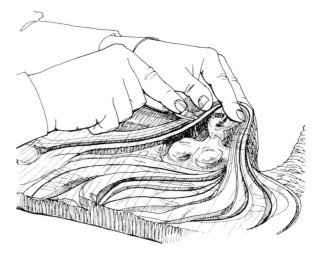

Finally go over the carving and crisp up the details with a razor-sharp knife.

attention to Eve's breasts, the apple and the snake by making them all nicely rounded and polished, and I have also made Eve's hair one of the most important pattern features. However, you might see Adam as being the centre of the design, in which case you could give him broad shoulders and a massive flowing beard – think about it. Finish working the whole carving – cutting in the flow of Eve's hair with the knife or V-tool, digging out the wood either side of Eve's neck with a spoon bit gouge, cutting in eye, mouth and nose details with the knife and so on.

Finishing

When you have carved and modelled all the motifs and characters and taken them as far as you want them to go it is time to work the final textures. Carve, sand and polish Adam, Eve and the snake; give Eve's hair a crisp undulating tooled finish and go over the trees and cut in a bark texture. Finally, brush down the whole carving and give it at least two coats of clear beeswax.

Hints, tips and afterthoughts

This project is deceptively difficult because of course you cannot suddenly become primitive or even work in a naïve manner and style. My advice is to keep it basic and bold. Work within your own limits and if you feel that the project is moving away from the primitive style it doesn't matter – carry on carving and leave the 'where did I go wrong?' inquiries for another day.

Thunderbird panel

The Indian tribes of the north west coast of British Columbia – the Tlingit, Haida, Tsimshian, Kwakiutl, Nootka and Salish – were unique in that they had what might be described as a wood-based culture. Where else could a society be found that spent about nine months of the year working, carving and

painting wood? These tribes were fortunate in that they were able to obtain an easy living both from the cedar forests and from the seas. There were bountiful supplies of salmon, otter, seal and beaver, and the food for the year was hunted, preserved and stored away in only a few months. What to do with the rest of the year? The Indians developed a very complex inter-tribal life-style that was in many ways

Inspirational design of a north west coast Indian wearing a traditional chilcat blanket and dance mask, all with characteristic motifs.

FRONT

BACK

SIDES

Inspirational designs of the back, front and side elevations of a carved and painted Tlingit box. Note the flattened and stylized patterns, designs and motifs.

Inspirational design of a carved and painted whale motif.

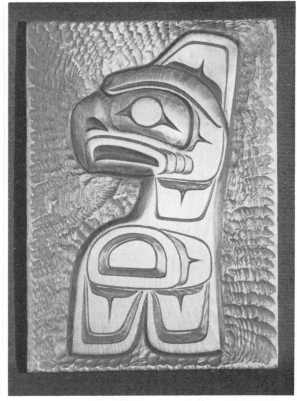

Thunderbird panel, carved by Kwakiutl Indian, Stan Matilpi from polished Cedar/Pine.

comparable to that of our European knights-of-old. Wars were won and lost, prisoners became slaves and there were tribal murders, feuds and battles. They had clans, noble families, secret societies and royalty with coats of arms, heraldic devices, mottos and crests which all took the form of carved and painted wood. The carvers worked through the long winter months making totem poles for the wealthy, treen for the Potlach (giving) ceremonies and boxes, canoes and house repairs. All were covered with characteristic relief-carved and painted designs and motifs such as sharks, bears and eagles; claws, wings, eyes, teeth and feathers.

Throughout the winter, the clans gathered in vast cedar-log halls to act out rituals and dance dramas developing themes of family ancestry and tribal myth. During many of these ceremonies gifts were exchanged such as carved boxes, plaques, dishes, spoons, masks, knives, fishing hooks, trays and rattles all of which were made of carved and painted wood. It was almost as if the whole society's wealth was expressed in woodworking.

Using the adze, the hooked or crooked knife and later the European gouge, the Indian craftsmen produced shallow relief carved items that were, and are, sophisticated in form and smooth to the touch. The carvings were worked in low-relief, brought to a fine finish and then painted with primary earth colours. If you look closely at the illustrated carving you will see that the animals and forms are represented in a flat, almost modern, graphic style. The eagle, bear or raven, for example, can be seen in front, side and plan views and all the areas in between are filled with parts of the animal such as claws and eyes. The Indian carvers developed a system in which the animals were divided into the basic elements. Once you know the symbols used, it is possible to look at a characteristic west coast Indian carving and read the mythical and heraldic designs and motifs.

Method
Shallow relief carving

Working time
6–8 hours, depending on tools and wood type

Tools and materials
For this step by step project carved in the Kwakiutl or Tlingit Indian style, you can use knives, gouges or both. If you have a good look at the illustrated panel you will see that, rather like on a wood engraver's block, the motifs are

Working drawing – the grid scale is four squares to 1in. Note the grain direction.

1"

GRAIN

made up of shallow relief V-section cuts, smooth surface plateaux and gently sloping planes that fall away into the V-cuts. You are therefore going to need a couple of small blade, hand knives plus maybe a V-gouge and a small U-shaped, scoop gouge. If you fancy working with a purpose-made chip knife, have a trial run before you go to any great expense.

Traditionally, Kwakiutl and Tlingit wood carvings were worked in Yew and Cedar, but almost any smooth grained, tight-textured and knot-free wood is suitable. You could try Yew, Cedar, Lime, Holly, Sycamore or even Poplar – it all depends on costs and availability. I suggest that you visit a supplier and try out as many off-cuts as possible and then settle for a wood that suits your needs. My personal choice of wood is Lime, not because it is traditional, but because it is still relatively cheap, easy to find and very pleasant to work. If you look at our squared-up drawing showing how to design and cut the panel, you will see that it is about $4\frac{1}{2}$in × 6in. There is of course no reason why you can't work the project larger or smaller.

Holding the piece of wood while you work is again a matter of personal choice. The north west coast Indians worked panels of this character on low benches, on the ground or even hand-held depending on the size and the scale of the piece. Sometimes the carver had an arrangement rather like a boot-mender's bench which was a loop of rope that went up through a hole in the work surface, over the wood to be worked and then down through another hole, all being kept taught with either a twist stick or the weight of the carver's foot. You need to be able to turn the wood continuously as you are working, so the clamp or holdfast needs to be flexible. We suggest that you either use a bench stop and the weight of your forearm, or screw the piece to a low bench or work donkey so that you can work and move around it. If you choose to knife-work on a very small panel it would be best to hold and manoeuvre the wood in one hand while you guide and work the knife with the other.

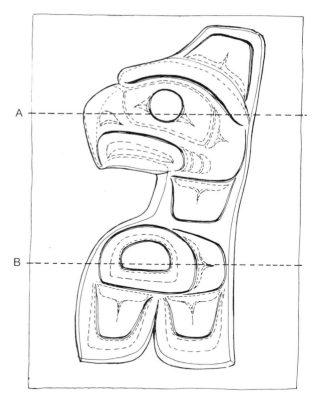

Pencil in the main lines of the design and work out which areas have to be V-cut.

Setting out the design

With a soft pencil and a piece of good quality tracing paper, draw up the design so that it fits the piece of wood that you have in mind. Take up the wood and look over it thoroughly, assessing the direction of the grain, twists, knots, splits and faults and then decide just how the motif is going to fit the wood and be worked.

Before going any further take a flat U-gouge and, working across the grain, remove a skim of surface wood. This will not only get you in the mood, but it will also show you how the wood is going to behave and leave you with a most beautiful and perfect working surface – slightly rippled and silky smooth to the touch. Take the design and pencil press transfer the lines on to the wood.

First cuts

From the illustrations you will see that most of the shapes need to be outlined with shallow and curved V-cuts. If you are using a knife,

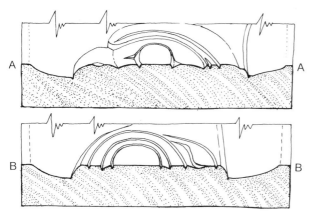

Cross sections on A–A and B–B showing the V-cuts and shallow relief areas.

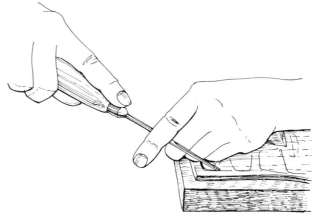

Cut-in the motifs with a V-tool.

Cut-in the lines of the design with the knife and cut away the unwanted ground with a scoop gouge.

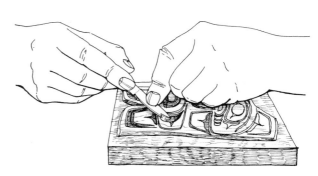

Cut away the sloping areas with the knife and use the initial V-cuts as stop-cuts.

there are at least two ways of working. You can either hold the knife in your right hand, rather like a dagger, and pull it towards you across the wood while the fingers of the other hand support and guide the blade; or you can hold it in one hand, rather like a pen, while you guide and push it away from you with the other. In either case, the aim is to work V-section outlines with the first cuts around the motif. The initial cut must follow the outline while the second must be angled into the first. If you are working correctly, a thin sliver of wood should fall away leaving a V-section. If however, you choose to work with a V-section gouge, just push and manoeuvre the gouge with one hand and support and guide it with the other – the wood should fall away at a single stroke.

Removing the ground

When you have cut-in and worked the main lines of the design you can start to remove and lower the surrounding ground. If you look at the photograph you will see that the ground has been chopped out with a scoop gouge. Wherever possible work steadily across the grain lowering the ground wood by about $\frac{1}{8}$in. Don't try and take the wood to a fine finish, just aim for a surface that shows off the direct and clean strokes of the gouge.

Cutting the fine lines of the motif

This whole project depends on the depth and width of various V-section cuts. If you make a cut, straight down into a piece of wood, and then slide a knife or gouge at an angle into this cut thereby removing a thin slice of wood, you

Two details.

will finish up with a smooth slope or angled plane. By doing this repeatedly the V-section cut will become deeper and wider. In many ways the procedure is similar to chip carving, but instead of repeatedly chopping into the wood and removing single chips, you slide the knife or gouge around the shapes removing thin curls of wood.

One or two areas are a little bit tricky and need some care, so you will have to keep your wits about you. For example, the outer eye is cut-in and then worked at an angle towards the inner eye. You do have to be very careful and make sure that you don't damage the sharp lines and the areas of delicate short grain. It all sounds rather complicated, but you will find that as you work, the Kwakiutl and Tlingit designs follow well defined rules that govern the carving. For example, eye centres are always in high relief and beaks and feathers are always represented by V-sections that cut straight down into the wood and then slope gently out. The main areas of the design should end up as bands of wood that stand up in high relief, almost like European strap carving. With a panel of this size and character, you will find that the cuts never need to be deeper than $\frac{1}{4}$in.

Painting the carving

Traditionally Kwakiutl Indian carvings were painted with primary stains and colours — reds, blues, black and white. The colours always followed and filled in the lines of the carved designs, the effect being to emphasize the shapes of the motifs and the depth of the cuts. If you decide to paint your carving, apply the paint so that the lines and forms are hard-edged, smooth and crisp. When the paint is dry, just break the surface with a fine sandpaper and then apply several coats of wax.

Hints, tips and afterthoughts

If, after a few minutes work, your hands feel sore it's not a bad idea to protect pressure areas with sticky plaster.

The moment your knife starts to cut roughly give it a few strokes on the stone – a dozen cuts followed by a stroke on the stone should suffice. In this way your carving will stay crisp and clean cut.

Carving in
the Round

American decoy duckling

Decoy ducks are imitation ducks used to lure wild fowl into cages or gun traps. The word 'decoy' comes from the Dutch words kooj and koye, meaning to lure, trap, entice or snare. Decoy usage is relatively straight forward – the duck shooter sits in his punt-like boat surrounded by wood carved and painted duck shaped decoys. Along comes a flock of wild duck, they see what they think are ducks at rest and make ready to settle on the water. Up pops the hunter, gun and all, bang! bang! . . . and instantly there are dead birds for the pot. Wilson's *American Ornithology* published about 1812, describes a typical hunter, punt and duck decoy set-up, 'Five or six wooden figures, cut and painted so as to represent ducks, and sunk, by pieces of lead nailed on their bottoms, so as to float at the usual depth on the surface, are anchored in a favourable position. The appearance of these usually attracts passing flocks, which alight and are shot down. Sometimes eight or ten of these painted wooden ducks are fixed on a wooden frame in various swimming postures, and are secured to the bow of the gunners skiff.' By all accounts decoys were successful, in fact so much so that by 1920, wild fowl populations were at risk and restrictions were placed on the use of decoys.

Traditional decoys come in a great many shapes, colours, sizes, materials and types – roughly carved, beautifully painted, hollow wood, metal, plastic, canvas and so on. However, as far as we are concerned, decoys are solid wood, gouge and rasp worked, unpainted sculptural forms that relate to, and are inspired by, American folk carvings.

Method
Carving in the round and whittling

Working time
5–8 hours

Decoy Duckling (made by the author). Waxed Pine with hardwood eyes and head dowel.

Inspirational designs **A**. Pintail Drake **B**. Canadian
Goose **C**. Drake Decoy **D**. Goose.

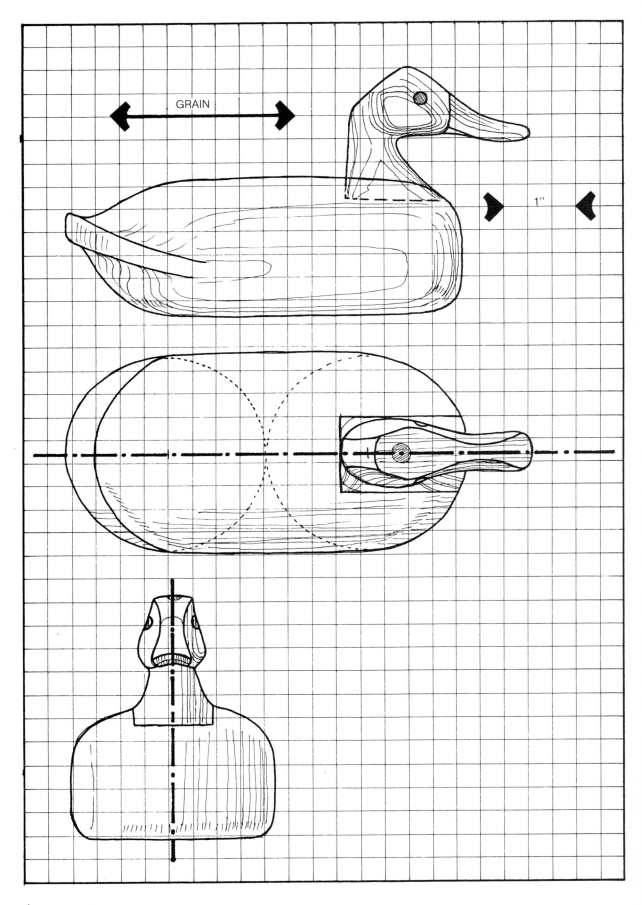

GRAIN

1"

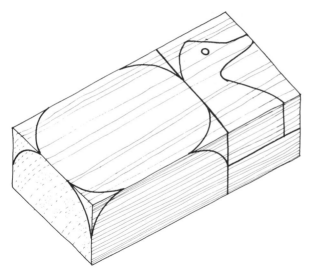

Take the 9in × 3in × 2½in piece of wood, allow 6in for the body and 3in for the head and set out the design.

Take the 6in × 3in × 2½in block of wood and with the coping saw, spokeshake and rasp make an upside-down boat shape. Note that the arrows indicate the direction of cut.

Tools and materials

Traditional decoys were made in two parts, the body and the head. The body was first of all roughed out of a bit of Pine, Cedar or some such local wood, with an axe or adze, and then taken to completion with a drawknife or spokeshave. The decoy heads were swiftly cut to shape with a bow saw and then whittled with a knife. Finally the head was fixed to the

Working drawing – the grid scale is three squares to 1in. Note the grain direction, the position of the head fixing dowel, and the tilt of the tail.

Take the surform and with the boat shaped block of wood in the vice, tail end uppermost, shape and work the tilt of the tail.

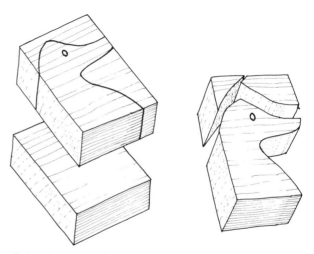

Take the piece of head wood, split it in half and then cut away the unwanted wood.

body with a nail or dowel and the whole carving was then rubbed down and painted.

For this project you need to use a light coloured Pine or similar wood – look for a piece that is about 9in long, 3in wide and 2½in thick. A piece of builder's rough timber, such as an off-cut from the end of a joist or rafter, would be perfect.

Cut the 9in length of wood into two pieces, one at 6in and the other at 3in. For tools, you need a coping or bow saw, a rasp, a drawknife or spokeshave, a straight gouge, a sharp knife and such items as sandpaper, a hand drill, pencil and ruler.

Note: If you want to make a life sized duck, then double up all the measurements.

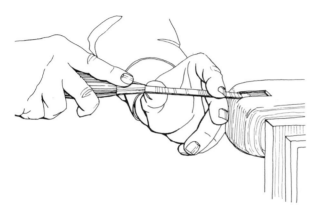

With a flat chisel cut a 1in wide, 1¾in long and ⅜in deep mortise in the duck body.

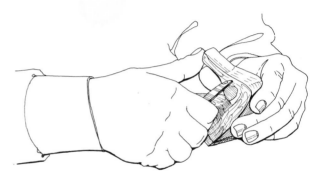

Check that the head is a good fit in the body and then with the knife bring the head to a good smooth finish.

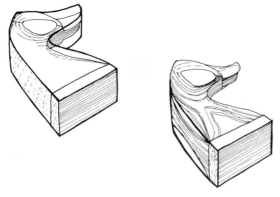

Rasp the duck's neck so that it tenons into the body mortise and then whittle the head to a direct and swift finish.

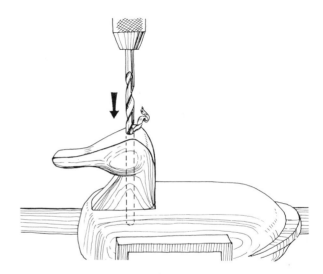

Fit the neck tenon into the body mortise and with a ⅜in bit drill down through the duck's head and into the body. Glue the head and eye dowels, rub down the wood until it is silky smooth and finally give the whole sculpture three coats of varnish.

Setting out the design: the body

Take the 6in length of wood, draw out the basic body lines and cut out the blank with the coping or bow saw, as illustrated. You should now have a piece of wood that is rounded at each end like two half circles. Label it *top, side, tail* and so on. Put the flat boat-shaped block, long side up in the vice, and set to work shaping it with the drawknife or spokeshave. Aim to reduce the long, top and side angles so that the wood looks like an upside-down rowboat. Now with the rasp, shape the wood at the front and tail so that the whole block sits on a flat base, but is otherwise nicely rounded.

The tail

Put the rounded, boat-shaped block of wood in the vice so that the tail end is uppermost then pencil in the angled lines of the tail as illustrated. Now with the saw and rasp reduce the bulk of wood at the top and bottom of the tail so that it angles up from the main body of the duck and stands out proud by about ½in as in the working drawing.

The body mortise

Place the decoy body, top side up in the vice, mark out a centre line and then cut and work a 1in wide, 1¾in long and ⅜in deep mortise, as illustrated. At this stage, don't worry about tidying up the mortise or making an absolute fit, just cut the wood crisply and be careful that you don't drive the chisel too deep which would split the wood.

Carving the head and fitting the head tenon

Take the 3in length of wood and mark out the side profile of the duck head as shown in the working drawing – the grain of the wood runs from the back of the head to the tip of the beak. Put the wood in the vice and with the coping saw cut out the head blank or profile. Work up the back of the head, around the face, along the top of the beak, under the beak tip and then curve down to the neck and throat. Try to keep the saw blade at 90° to the working face of the wood and take extra care when you come to the tight angles and turns. When you have cut out the head blank, take the rasp and reduce the neck tenon so that it's a snug fit in the body mortise. Finally, take the sharp knife and whittle the duck head to a swift finish.

Finishing

When the head tenon and body mortise are a comfortable fit and the overall head shape has been whittled, take the hand drill and bore a $\frac{3}{8}$in hole down through the duck's head, through the neck and into the body. Also while you have the drill to hand, bore two $\frac{1}{4}$in holes for the eyes and make hardwood dowels to fit. Arrange all the parts, glue the mortise, tenon and dowels and then put the whole thing together, as shown. When the glue is dry, cut off all the dowel ends so that they are flush with the main body of the wood and then, with a series of graded sandpapers, rub down the whole sculpture. Work the wood until it is silky smooth to the touch and then give it at least three coats of clear varnish, drying and rubbing down between coats.

Hints, tips and afterthoughts

When you are working the decoy with gouge and rasp, try to achieve a form that has flowing lines and a total absence of tool marks.

When you come to the glueing, use a white PVA wood glue and if you decide to paint the duck, use flat colours protecting them with a matt varnish.

Netsuke mouse

Kamakura and Kyoto were traditionally the most important centres of woodcarving in old Japan, turning out fine products for the imperial courts and palaces. Of course, most of the woodcarvers worked on the straight forward utilitarian items of everyday life – bowls, dishes, kitchen and farm equipment, but carvers who were really skilled tended to concentrate their talents on making the uniquely Japanese, wonderfully sensitive carvings known as netsuke. Netsuke (Net'su ka), meaning small carvings worn or attached to various articles, such as a button or toggle, were primarily used to fasten boxes, pipes and tobacco pouches to a man's kimono sash. However, when in the nineteenth century laws banned the common people from wearing jewellery, gradually the netsuke became an important item of adornment and prestige. Traditional netsukes are characterized by being very small, usually only an inch or so in diameter, and depicting friendly animals, beasts and figures – all pierced, undercut, incised and intricately detailed. The netsuke carvers used slender, flexible bladed chisels which they worked pen-like in one hand, while they turned and held the wood with the other.

Towards the end of the nineteenth century, Japan was opened up to the west, and in a very short time dress fashions changed and netsukes became obsolete. The woodcarvers of course had no choice but to adapt to the changes, so they used their skills to make trade carvings such as boxes, buttons and chessmen. From that time to this, the Japanese wood-carvers have had to continually modify their style and methods of working to suit changing needs. Generally speaking, however, they still work within the spirit of the netsuke tradition, their carvings remaining small, sensitive, humorous, delicate and intricate – little figures, birds, animals and flowers; all

Japanese netsuke mouse.

beautifully worked with expressive tool marks and considered, fine details.

Method
Carving in the round

Working time
3–8 hours

Tools and materials
For this project you will most certainly need to use a super-fine smooth wood – what better than a piece of butter coloured Box? This wood is extremely close, even and dense in its grain, and when crisply cut, it appears to have a natural polish. You might have to search around for just the right piece, but see if you can get a 3in × 3in × 3in cube of English wood.

For tools you need a set of super-sharp miniature gouges (I use a set made by Henry Taylor), a fine blade knife, a coping saw, a rasp, plastercine and, of course, scraps of paper, pencils, compass and a measure.

Setting out the design
If you have a look at the illustrated mouse, you will see that it fits very snugly within a nut-shaped or ball form. Start by taking your cube of wood and the compass and mark off all six faces with 3in diameter circles. Now with the coping saw and rasp, work the wood until it is smooth and spherical. Making the ball is tricky – you must work the wood corner by corner and watch out for the direction of the grain. Aim to make a smooth nut of wood that fits comfortably in your hand. Of course, if you are really keen and fancy a challenge you could work a very small mouse, say 1in in diameter, but think carefully about it.

Making a plastercine maquette
Make a 3in ball of plastercine and mark it off as *back*, *front*, *top* and *side* and look at the working drawings and photograph to see how the mouse fits the ball form. If you can't quite see how, for instance, the feet or tail work in relationship to each other, then make a little plastercine mouse and actually curl him into a ball. See how the tail wraps over the shoulder and around the neck and how the feet, ears, nose and eyes are set and detailed. When you have made a satisfactory working model, put it out of harm's way but within easy reach; pin up as many magazine clips and mouse studies as you can find and arrange the tools comfortably to hand.

Marking out and first cuts
Take the ball of wood and a soft pencil and carefully draw in the lines of the mouse. At this stage don't even try to detail the feet or anything else – it is much better to concentrate on the big generous curve of the tail, the hump of the spine and the other main forms. When the guide lines have been drawn in, take the ball of wood in one hand, hold the knife as if you are going to pare an apple and then cut-in the lines of the design with a series of V-cuts. As you work, keep the ball turning and continue to pivot and control the knife with your thumb keeping a close watch on the direction of the grain.

Working drawing – the grid scale is four squares to 1in. Note the grain direction runs from base to head.

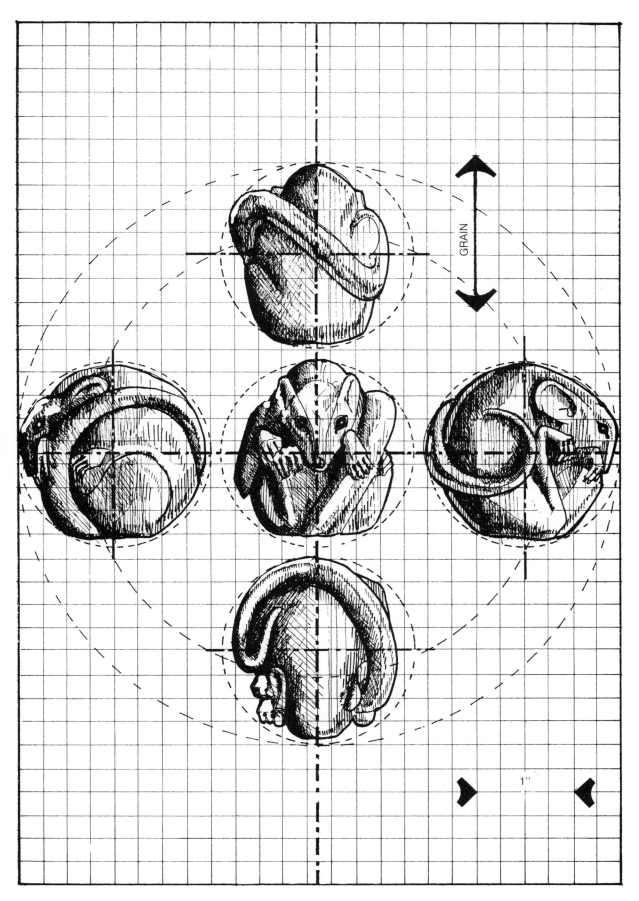

GRAIN

1"

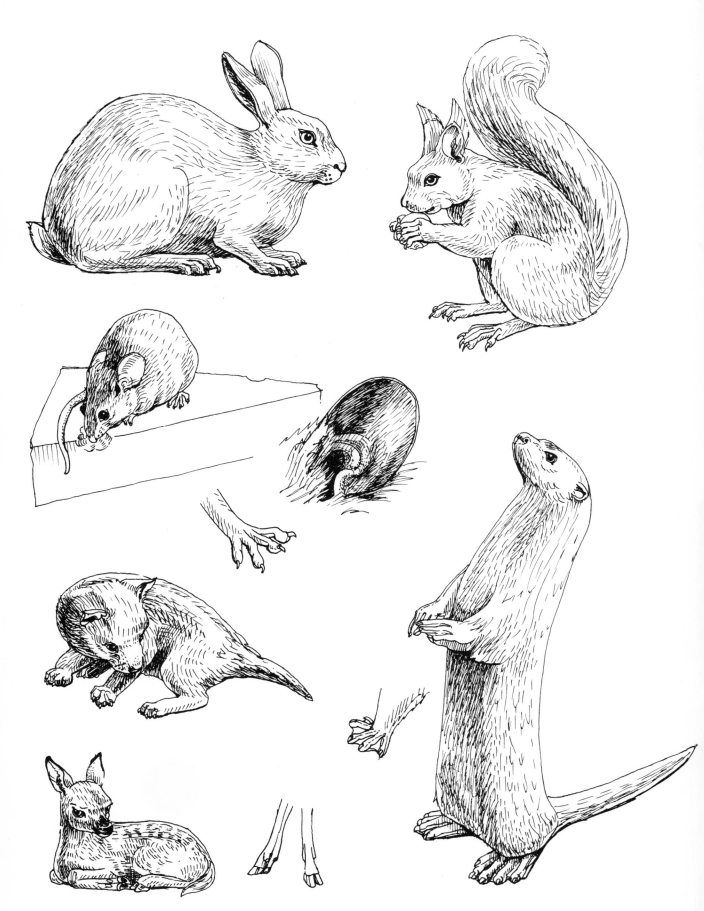

Inspirational design. Before you start this project study as many mouse pictures as possible.

Cutting-in and modelling

Still with the wood in one hand and the knife or miniature tool in the other, carve the wood using the V-trenches as stop-cuts. Pare and pull the knife towards you, all the time lowering the unwanted ground and cutting into the stop-cuts. Every few minutes, put the wood down alongside the plastercine maquette and stand back to assess your progress. Is the hump of the tail standing

Study forms and details and maybe carve a larger animal such as a rabbit or squirrel. It's always a good idea with a project of this character to make a sketchbook of ideas and details.

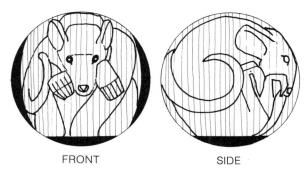

FRONT   SIDE

Once you have made a few sketch drawings and maybe made a plastercine working maquette, take your cut and rasped ball of box wood and draw in the various views.

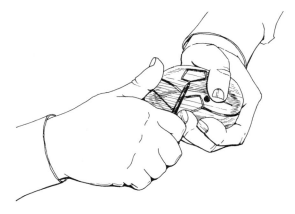

With a sharp knife, cut-in the lines of the design with a series of V-section cuts.

proud? Can you see the curve of the spine? Is the head going to fit within the wood? Are you cutting too deep? You must continually check and question your carving. Try not to work on a single area such as an eye or paw – it is much better to keep the wood turning and moving and carve the whole form.

With a project of this size and character, the main difficulty is not carving the individual features but keeping the overall form neatly balanced and achieving the final statement that says *mouse*.

Finishing

When you feel that you have taken the carving as far as it is going to go having carved and detailed the toes, ears, mouth, eyes and the rest, sharpen up your knife or tool, and go over the whole mouse cutting in the fine hair texture. Finally, take a piece of the finest grade sandpaper and just touch the pad of the nose

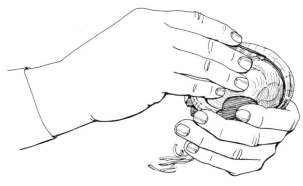

Using the V-section cuts as stop-cuts carve and pare the bold forms.

Continue lowering some areas of wood and modelling others.

Finally, with a knife or fine V-tool go over the finished carving and cut-in the hair texture.

and the rims of the ears to take the wood to a smooth finish.

Hints, tips and afterthoughts

When you are buying Box wood, watch out that you buy the real thing. Avoid central American or West Indian Box wood, because it is liable to split and cut-up with a dull and off-yellow hue – go for home-grown wood.

If you find as you work, that the wood is difficult to hold, or your hands are blistered, sore or damp, wear a pair of soft chamois-leather dress gloves.

When you are cutting the hair texture, make sure that the little nicks are organized so that they follow and emphasize the form.

English Renaissance cherub

It has been said that the Golden Age of English woodcarving started about 1750 and finished about 1850, and there's no doubt about it – this hundred year period was remarkable for the fertility of its artists, designers and woodcarvers. The fashion was for lavish, larger than life realism – masses of carved and gilded fruit, giant swags of flowers and rather bouncy roly-poly cherubs. It must have been a fantastic time for woodcarvers, with every designer, artist and rich follower of fashion, clamouring for unrestrained crêches of angels, children, sweet babies, winged heads and celestial spirits. If you are new to woodcarving I am sure you are wondering just how it's possible to carve such detail. The answer is simply through using Lime wood. The book *Timbers For Woodworkers* published by Evans Brothers in 1947, says of Lime, 'The timber produced is valuable in a few respects. It is of a yellowish colour, light in weight, close grained and cuts evenly in every direction. Its utilisation for carving is not so great as in former years when this art was so much appreciated.' That is indeed a cool and correct understatement – Lime, as far as I am concerned, is a miracle wood. It cuts and works like no other, it smells sweet and is soft and cool to the touch.

Next time you get the chance to visit a grand house of the late seventeenth or early eighteenth centuries, search out the wood-carving and peer closely at the wall panels and over-mantels. Marvel at the silk-smooth, deeply undercut angels of Grinling Gibbons and the soft, cheeky cherubs of Edmund Carpenter. Enjoy the flowing lines and the sensuous forms of the woodcarving, but also, if possible, let your finger tips run over and

Inspirational design of the Virgin and Child, fifteenth century, Dutch.

Inspirational design of a detail from a relief in the church of St. Francesco, Florence, carved in the fifteenth century by Agostino Di Duccio.

Inspirational design of a mirror frame carved by Panciera Besarel of Venice.

under the carved figures. Feel the crisp tool marks and see how the gouges and spoon chisels have worked the deep undercuts. Once you have taken in the whole depth and span of the work, look closer and closer still and let your eyes see beyond the layers of gilt, dust and wax. Look especially for skilfully built-up

areas, laminated wood and painstakingly glued and carved arms, legs and wings. An aged woodcarver once told me that seventeenth and eighteenth-century woodcarvings were made up in equal parts of divine inspiration, worldly perspiration, clever know-how and Lime wood.

Method
Carving in the round and undercutting

Working time
6–7 days

Tools and materials
For a project of this size and character you are going to need a $\frac{1}{2}$in shallow-curve, straight gouge, a couple of small spoon gouges, say $\frac{1}{8}$in and $\frac{1}{2}$in, a small knife and either a dog-leg chisel or a flat spoon-bit chisel. And of course you will need a bench stop or clamp, a coping saw and such items as a measure, pencil, rifflers and sandpaper. I've seen students working this project with just about every known woodcarving tool from a curious

Seventeenth-century cherub carved by Edmund Carpenter for Sir John Brownlow. Worked in Lime wood and waxed.

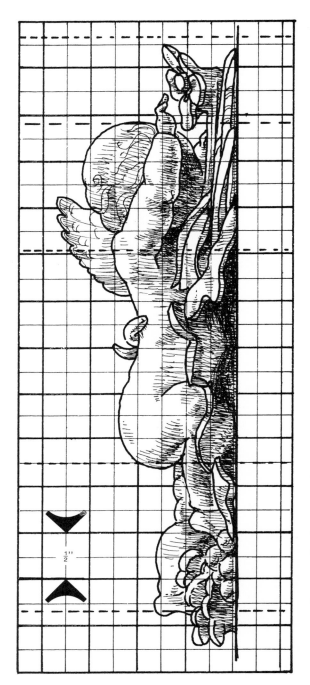

Working drawing – the grid scale is two squares to $\frac{1}{2}$in.

rosewood and ivory handled left-corner, spoon-bit to a nineteenth-century silver handled surgeon's bone chisel. So don't worry if you haven't got just the tools, as listed, use the tools you have got and try to adjust the cutting techniques as you go along.

Note: A quality tool will last you a life time. Save up, find out your needs and then buy the best.

For this project you must use Lime. Find a piece that measures 8in along the grain, 4in across and $2\frac{1}{2}-3$in deep (see the design and cut working drawing the scale of which is $\frac{1}{2}-\frac{3}{4}$in between the arrows). Before you start this project take a good look at the photograph. If you feel that you want to concentrate on the cherub and leave the flowers and leaves or if

you would prefer to work the project larger, then this is the time to get a bigger piece of wood, adjust the working drawing and change the scale to, say, $\frac{3}{4}-1$in per grid square.

Working drawing – the grid scale is two squares to $\frac{1}{2}$in. Note the direction of the grain and the fact that the wings are built-up.

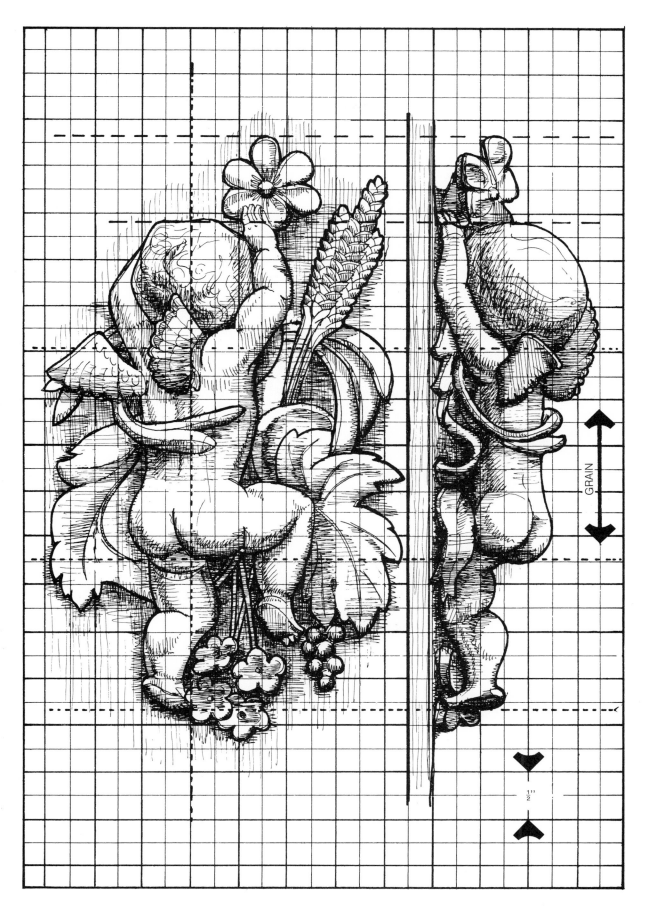

GRAIN

$\frac{1''}{2}$

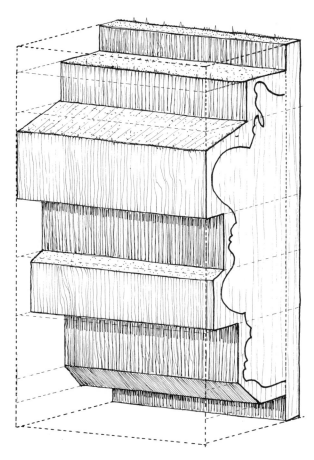

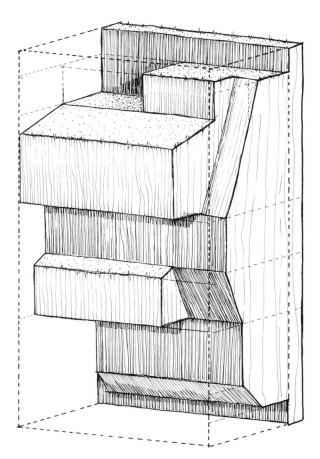

Once you have established the main lines of the design, clear away the unwanted wood with a saw and chisel.

Block out the main forms of head, arms, buttocks, etc.

Setting out the design

Take one last look at the block of Lime checking it for splits, small loose knots and all the other nasties that are just waiting to sneak up on careless woodcarvers. If on consideration you think the wood is badly coloured, or the grain is twisted, then now is the moment to find another piece.

When you are happy with your wood, take a pencil, sketch pad and a good quality sheet of tracing paper and start to carefully draw out the cherub, adjusting the overall design as you think fit. Pencil press the traced lines onto the various faces of the wood and when the complete design has been transferred heavily pencil and block in the main forms and areas of wood that have to be chopped out. It's not a bad idea at this stage to clearly label the wood *top*, *side*, *head* and so on since you will then be less likely to make a mistake and, say, chop off

an area of foot or arm – it's easily done!
Note: Beware of felt tip pens which can mark, bleed and stain light coloured woods.

First cuts

Place the wood squarely face-up on the work surface and with a coping or bow saw, a mallet and a straight chisel, start to remove the main blocks of unwanted wood. Establish the important parts of the cherub, the head, arms, buttocks and so on, but do be very careful that you don't split the wood along the grain or chop-in too deep. As you continue cutting away wood, keep re-pencilling in the main points of reference.

Roughing out

Take up the straight gouge, and with the wood held securely in a vice or clamp, start to shape up the form. Chop off the corners and sharp angles and gradually cut around and across the grain of the wood until you begin to find the high points of the cherub – the back of the head and the buttocks. I find that Lime is very easily cut and worked with the gouge being held in one hand and guided, pushed and manoeuvred with the other. If, however, your hands begin to feel bruised and tired then use a mallet. By the time you have chopped out the rough and generally rounded up the cherub at the waist, legs, head, shoulders and bottom, the shape will begin to look lifelike and realistic. It's really exciting when the carving starts to come out of the wood. But don't stop – just continue to work the wood little by little. Always try to cut across the grain but if you have to cut with the grain, take care not to let your tool run into the wood and splinter off.

Undercutting and lowering the ground

When you have reached a point where the form is rounded and the main shapes are well defined and organized, then you can start to undercut the cherub and generally clean up and lower the unwanted ground wood. With the spoon gouge and the dog-leg chisel or flat spoon-bit, cut away the wood that links the cherub to the base. The carving action at this point is – straight down into the wood with the flat spoon-bit, chop at an angle into the initial cut and then scoop out the angle of waste wood. Cut, chop, scoop and pare, cut, chop, scoop and pare – all the time working around and under the cherub and getting closer to the final form. As you carve the limbs, arms and head and reveal more of the smooth podgy roundness of the Cherub, you will have to keep lowering the ground-wood. Chop down with the flat spoon-chisel and then slide and cut out the waste wood with the curved gouge or the dog-leg.

Note: See the Grinling Gibbons flower for the leaves and flowers.

Continue cutting away the wood that surrounds the little figure, all the time rounding the form and increasing the undercuts.

Finishing

The cherub needs to be silky smooth, so when

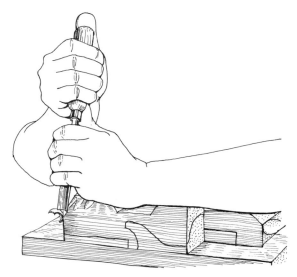

Once you have blocked out the wood, take a straight gouge and start to model the forms.

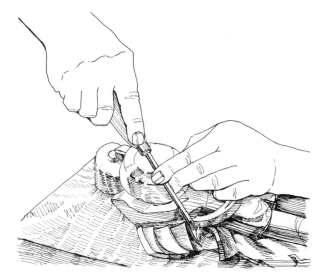

Having generally rounded the shapes you can start to lower the ground and undercut with a flat spoon bit gouge.

you have tooled the form to a good finish start to go over the wood with a file, riffler and graded sandpaper. Hold the sandpaper in your fingers or palm, not in a block, and gently work over the form, feeling out the subtle dips and curves. When the overall feel and finish is just right, take a small knife and clean up the little creases behind the knees, buttocks and toes. The wings can be whittled out of a couple of pieces of off-cut Lime, brought to a tooled finish and then cut-in to the shoulders and glued, trimmed and finished until they look

Use tools that suit the work in hand, so for small creases take a knife and carve with a series of sliding, shaping V-cuts.

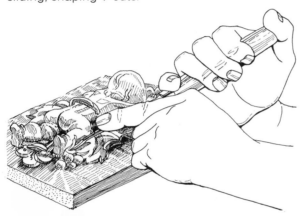

Use fine gouges to do the delicate details and undercuts.

The wings can be whittled out of off-cuts.

like a growing part of the whole. Finally, the cherub needs to be polished – no stain, varnish or sealer, just apply the wax, a little at a time, and keep rubbing away with a fluff-free cloth until the wood takes on a clean, yellow shine.

Hints, tips and afterthoughts
When you are working on short grain areas

such as the fingers, the top of the head and the heels, be very careful not to force the tool, always stroke and shave the wood. There is a point, just after the form has been roughed out, when beginners tend to loose heart and wish they had taken up golf or gardening. Don't be put off if at this stage the whole project looks a mess, just spend ten minutes sharpening up your tools and then get back to work! If your back, shoulders or arms start to ache, try changing the height of the work surface, sitting on a stool or standing back and re-assessing your progress and giving your muscles a rest.

Always have your working drawings, photographs and inspirational drawings to hand, then you won't loose touch with the project.

Indian totem bowl
When western travellers and artists discovered the arts and crafts of north America in the eighteenth and nineteenth centuries and for the first time saw and handled Indian carved totem poles, carved and painted dishes, carved food bowls, dance masks, carved chests and the like – they were amazed. Although these carvings were faultlessly worked they were so strange and outside the thinking of western European art and design that they were labelled Primitive and then tucked away into odd corners of private collections. This lack of understanding continued all through the nineteenth century with the majority of so called primitive woodcarvings being burnt by missionaries, banned by the authorities and generally despised by artists and craftsmen. This sorry state of affairs suddenly changed in the early years of this century when revolutionary artists such as Picasso, Braque and Matisse, who were trying to break away from classical Greek and Roman art forms, declared that the tribal, New World arts were both new and modern. Today most of us realize that tribal, ethnic and primitive art forms are significant, unique and meaningful in their

own right and best appreciated when they are not compared to our own traditional arts and crafts.

The biggest wooden sculptures ever carved were made by the Indians that lived along the north west coast of north America (see the Thunderbird panel). They shaped the giant red cedar trees with two of the oldest wood working tools known to man – the adze and the crooked/hooked knife and it is no overstatement to say that as woodcarvers they were beyond compare. Carved and painted totem poles over 70 feet high; steamed, bent, pegged, carved and painted chests; adze and knife worked canoes; dishes, masks, caskets and poles – all carved with almost unbelievable skill and care.

These north west coast Columbian Indians lived in what can only be described as a woodcarvers paradise. The seas to the west gave them unlimited food and in a few months they were able to gather, preserve and store enough food for the rest of the year. Once the food was stored away the Indians withdrew into themselves, names were changed, masks were worn and long dance dramas and spiritual ceremonies were performed. During this supernatural period it was necessary to wear wood carved and painted masks and exchange gifts of carved dishes and bowls and to carve the huge heraldic totems. Working with adze and knife the Tlingit, Kwakiutl, Tsimshian and Haida Indians cut, worked and carved the virgin cedars. Building, steaming, laminating, jointing and carving, the Indians made just about everything from wood – domestic bowls, ceremonial boxes, cooking boxes, masks, puppets and hats. Even cloaks and kilts were made of cedar bark.

The Indians developed a peculiar carved motif system with the names of the clans and the dance drama beasts being shown as flat, relief carved and painted graphic symbols. For example a duck or bear food bowl would not only be worked in the round so that it looked duck or bear shaped, it would also be patterned and surface carved with flat, front and side view duck and bear motifs – eyes, claws,

Inspirational design of a nineteenth-century Haida village with characteristic totem poles and door posts.

feathers etc. Not only were the wood carvings functional and decorative in that they held food and were carved and painted, they also doubled up as totems that had mythological and clan meaning. The woodcarvings of these Indians has been described as stylized realism, and once the forms are understood, the clan motifs, myth figures and heraldic symbols can be read. For example, the Thunderbird has a curved beak and ears and gave man strength to build houses, the Eagle is almost the same but without ears and the raven has a straight beak.

Method
Carving in the round

Working time
6–8 days

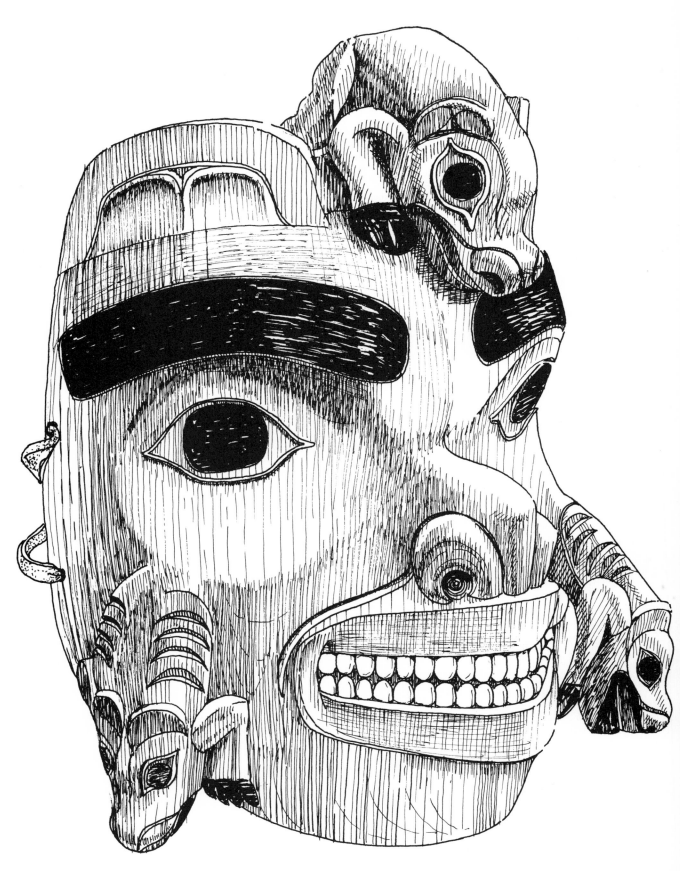

Inspirational design of a Tlingit sharman's bear mask made about 1860 and carved and painted.

A Haida animal headed bowl that has been carved and painted. Note the stylized motifs.

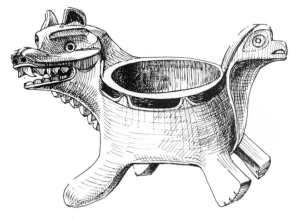

Nineteenth-century Kwakiutl wolf bowl.

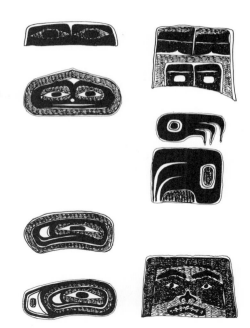

Inspirational designs for carved and painted eye, claw and face motifs.

Tools and materials

For this step by step project you are going to need a deep U-section scoop-gouge, a large wide U-section gouge, a small V-chisel, a chip carving knife or better still a crooked knife, a coping saw and such workshop items as a bench vice, pencils, riffler files, drills, calipers, a measure and plenty of sketch paper.

Before you start, carefully consider the task ahead and bear in mind that there are a great many ways of working wood. So if you find you carve well with, say, a crooked knife and a single gouge or an adze and an old kitchen knife then, these are the right tools for you. My advice is to have a trial run with as many tools as possible and you will then have some idea as to your needs. Traditionally, the Indian carvers used unseasoned Red Cedar which is green wood straight from the tree, but if you can't manage this I suggest that you visit a supplier and go for a wood that is smooth, fine grained and free from knots and splits. Maybe you could try American Basswood, Sycamore or Lime. You need a block of wood 10in long, 8in wide and 6in deep as illustrated in the design and cut diagram.

Setting out the design

Take your block of wood, look over it thoroughly, clean it and then set it fair and square on the work surface. Look at my photograph and the illustrations and see if you can feel your way around the shape and form of the bowl. When you are familiar with the various curves, lines and motifs you can then start to pencil sketch the elevations onto the faces of the block of wood. If, as you are drawing out the carving, you feel that the bowl could be deeper, longer or different in any other way adjust as you go. As a woodcarver there are two ways of seeing this project – you can either think of it as a piece of three-dimensional sculpture that just happens to be hollowed out or, like me, you can see it parimarily as a bowl that has bird characteristics.

Once the various views have been drawn out on the sides of the wood, you can begin to rough-out the form.

First cuts

With the coping saw, a large U-section gouge

American north west coast Indian bird-shaped bowl, carved, painted and polished.

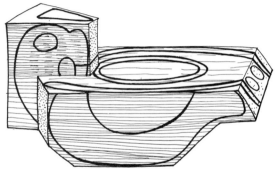

Draw out the design and with saw and gouge clear away the unwanted wood.

and the block of wood held secure in a vice or against a bench stop, you can start to clear away unwanted wood. When you have removed the main bulk of waste wood and established the rim level, the bowl centre and one or two other reference points, then you need to drill a pilot or depth hole. Measure the total thickness of wood from bowl rim to bowl base and then centre drill a guide hole. If you look at the squared drawing you will see that from rim to base the wood is about 3in thick – take a drill and work a hole that is no more than $2\frac{1}{2}$in deep. Mark clearly the thickness of the bowl walls and then begin to cut away the waste. Work from bowl rim to the centre of the guide hole and slowly remove long gouge-scoops of wood. Gradually work and gouge the bowl hollow, all the time assessing the thickness of the bowl wall and base.

Note: When you come to the bottom of the guide hole you should be $\frac{1}{2}$in short of the bowl base. If you have any doubts as to the amount of wood removed and remaining, leave it and go back to it at a later stage.

Working the bird form

With the coping saw, gouge and crooked knife begin to shape-up the bird form – the curve of the neck, the head and beak, the hole pierced between beak and neck and so on. Try to cut and work across and around the grain – never dig and lever with the tools or go straight along a grain line. As you work, keep the bowl moving and turning, all the while re-

When you have re-established the lines of the design, drill a pilot or depth hole at the centre of the bowl and work into it with a scoop gouge.

pencilling in the main areas, shapes and points of reference. After some considerable effort and toil you will arrive at a point where the bowl/bird form is near completion almost, as it were, hidden below the surface of the wood. Now is the moment to put down your tools, turn off the radio and stand back and have a

Working drawing – the grid scale is two squares to 1in. Note the direction of the grain.

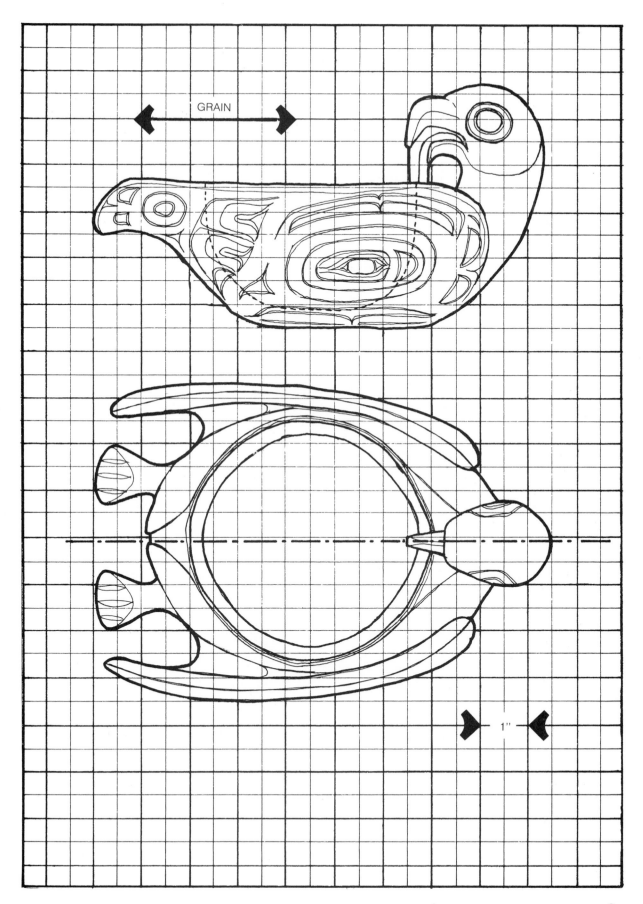

GRAIN

1"

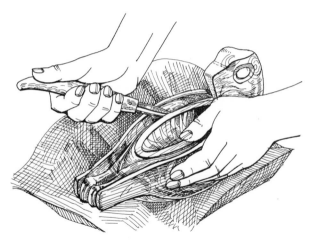

Support the bowl on an old cushion or sand bag and carve the areas that are difficult to reach between the wings with a fine gouge or crooked knife.

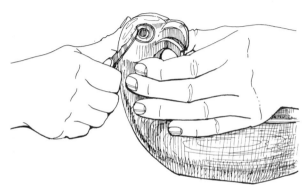

Finally go over the form with a sharp knife and cut-in the fine details and the rippled finish.

good look at the carving. Be very critical – is the beak right? Does the neck spring out of the body at the correct angle? Are the wings thin enough? All the time question the quality of the carving and your progress.

Finding the form

With every cut of the gouge or slice of the knife you will be getting closer to the bird form that sits just under the surface of the wood – take it easy and only remove the wood little by little. With this carving there are several tricky areas, for example, the beak and eye are not only delicate, short grained and

difficult to work but they are also two of the bird's most important characteristics. This being so, I suggest that you leave them as bulk wood and tackle them last.

As the bird comes out of the wood the carving will become so fragile that you will have to cradle it in your lap or on a sand bag and work on it with paring knife strokes.

When you are happy with the overall form and shape of the carving, go over it with a knife and give the surface a slightly rippled and tooled finish. Finally with a small knife and the smallest scoop-gouge you must cut in the various shallow relief-cut symbols and motifs (see the Thunderbird).

Hints, tips and afterthoughts

You will no doubt reach a point when decisions have to be made. Should you work on? Should you throw it all in the dustbin? Or should you settle for less than the best and call a halt? We all have these doubts – my advice is to put the carving out of sight for a day or two and then come back to it with a fresh eye.

Traditionally, this bowl would have been made with soft easily worked green wood and simple tools and I have no doubt that along the way the Indian carver would adjust his carving to suit the grain of the wood, hidden knots and splits, changes in needs and style, and so on. So don't be bound by initial ideas on just how the carving should look – always be prepared to veer away from my designs and to modify your work.

Question If I work with green wood, won't the bowl shrink and split?

Answer If you are working with found wood, let's say a piece of drift wood or a branch torn down in a storm, then you must expect difficulties – but there are also rewards. I once worked a bowl project with a piece of storm wood and every cut was a joy. At the end of the day the finished bowl didn't twist or warp at all.

Carving Furniture

Pennsylvanian German plate rack

In the last quarter of the seventeenth century William Penn and other English Quakers set up a colony in the area of the New World that is now known as Pennsylvania. Once settled, the liberal and tolerant Quakers encouraged other persecuted religious groups to join them. German settlement began in 1683 with a dozen or so families from the Mennonite sect and within a few years they were joined by the Amish, Dunkers and a great many other break-away religious and pietist groups.

The Pennsylvanian Dutch (a corruption of Deutsch) settlers were hard working, skilled and educated, so they were soon able to establish rich and prosperous farms; so much so that by the eighteenth century over a third of the population of Pennsylvania was German. However, right from the start they were a people apart since they didn't speak English, they held onto their religious beliefs and customs and, most important of all, they put all their energies into re-creating an Old World, German type society.

Inspirational designs for pattern, layout and design ideas for faceboards.

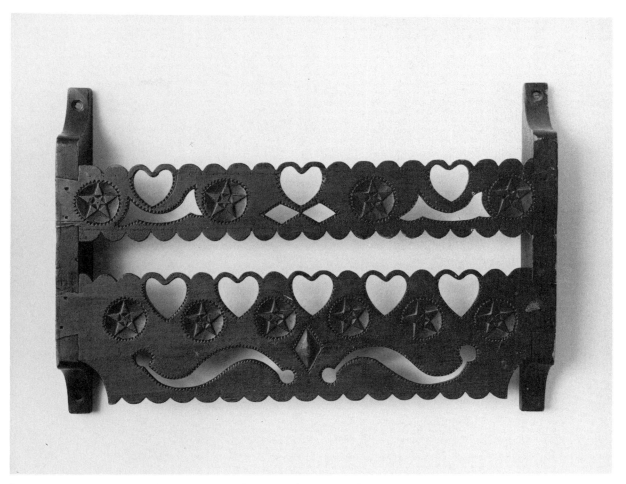

Early nineteenth-century Pennsylvanian German plate rack with pierced hearts and painted hex motifs.

This inward looking and rather isolated state of affairs resulted in what can only be described as a unique art, craft and furniture style. Chests and boxes decorated with bold, brightly painted flowers, swags and stars; chairs with pierced heart backs and seats and beds, tables and dressers all carved, pierced and painted with scrolls, scoops, scallops, diamonds, hearts and stars. Of all these beautifully carved and painted motifs the hex is really the most interesting.

In medieval Germany it was believed that devils on horseback (nightmares), rode through the night casting the evil eye and making mischief. It was also believed that the only way to stop these witches or hexen was to paint a ring of magic symbols – hex. Suddenly, in the eighteenth century the German settlers

revived the custom of painting and carving hex in a big way. Huge painted hex motifs on barn walls, hex patterns on cupboards, chairs and boxes – in fact, the craftsmen carved or painted a hex on just about every surface that could be decorated. I don't know for sure how, when or why the custom re-established itself, but I would guess that Red Indians, harsh storms, strange cattle, crop diseases and wild beasts made the settlers feel insecure and thought that a liberal scattering of hex might put things right. The hex motifs are usually characterized by bold geometrical symbols – usually stars, crosses, hearts and diamonds, enclosed by circles.

Method
Chip carving and piercing

Making time
2–3 days

Inspirational ideas for three simple hex designs.

GRAIN

1"

GRAIN

1"

Tools and materials

This project is ideal for raw beginners because it uses prepared timber, a few basic tools, simple techniques and, best of all, the end result is a very rewarding and usable cottage piece of furniture. You need five lengths of a straight grained, knot-free, prepared Parana Pine, two pieces 4in wide, 13in long and 1in deep; one piece 5in wide, 18 in long and $\frac{1}{2}$in deep; one piece 3in wide, 18in long and $\frac{1}{2}$in deep and one piece $4\frac{1}{2}$in wide, $16\frac{1}{2}$in long and $\frac{1}{2}$in deep.

Note: If you can only get prepared timber of $\frac{7}{8}$in rather than 1in or $\frac{3}{8}$in rather than $\frac{1}{2}$in, then this will be fine, but remember to adjust the design to fit.

For tools, you need a coping or fret saw, a small hand drill, a $\frac{1}{2}$in flat chisel, a $\frac{1}{2}$in straight gouge and such tools as a saw, compass, pencil, ruler, hammer, sandpaper and pins.

First steps

Start by sorting out and checking over the lengths of wood and making sure that they are free from warps, splits and dead knots. When you are happy that all is correct, take a last look at the cutting list and working drawings and then clearly pencil label the wood *end, shelf* and so on.

The ends

Take the 1in end-boards, square them up on the work surface and then mark out the shelf-end housing slots. With the wood secure in the vice, saw, chisel-cut and clear the open ended housing slots or trenches, as illustrated. When the trenches, one on each board, have been worked and you are sure they are a good fit take the tracing paper and pencil and set out the curves at the top and bottom of the end-boards. Now take the coping saw, rasp and sandpaper and work the curves until they are smooth and free from splinters, jags and sharp edges.

Working drawing and details – the working drawing grid scale is one square to 1in and the details are four squares to 1in. Note the dovetailed and pinned joints.

With a compass mark out the scalloped edge.

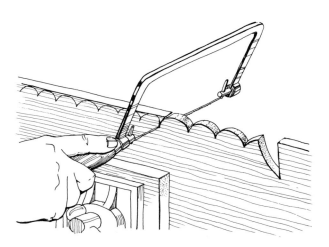

Secure the marked board in the vice and cut the scalloping with a coping saw.

Drill starter holes through the hearts and cut and work them with the coping saw.

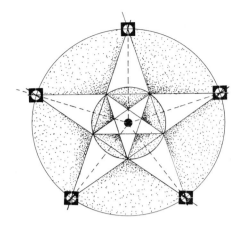

Use a compass and a protractor set at 72° to draw up the star in circle hex motifs. Note the darker shading at the edges of the star indicates the depth of carving – the darker the shading, the deeper the cut.

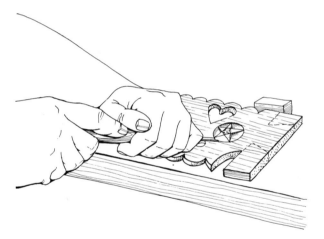

Once you have drawn out the hex motifs, lower the ground between the star points with a shallow gouge.

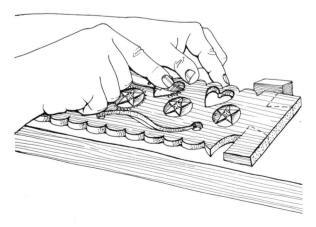

Cut the decorative nicks with a sharp knife.

The face boards

Take both boards and with pencil, tracing paper and a stack of rough paper, work and set-out the position of the pierced, carved and cut motifs.

The scalloping

If you look closely at the board edges on the photograph you will see that the scalloping is based on a series of linked, compass-drawn half circles. Set pencil lines $\frac{5}{8}$in away from the board edges, mark them off at 1in intervals, and then with the compass fixed at a radius of $\frac{1}{2}$in, draw up the row of half-circles, as illustrated. Once drawn, the scalloped edge can be cut and worked with the coping saw and then rubbed down with the sandpaper.

The pierced heart motifs

If you look at the heart shapes you will see that, top-to-tail, they fit into $1\frac{3}{4}$in × $1\frac{3}{4}$in squares. Take some rough paper, tracing paper and a pencil and draw-up and work on the motifs until they are plump, nicely rounded and symmetrical. Notice how the top cheeks of the hearts fit the 1in diameter grid of the scalloped half-circles leaving delicate and slender bridges of wood. It is most important that these bridges are no narrower than $\frac{1}{4}$in. Once you have established the shape and position of the hearts and you have double checked just how they work in relationship to the rest of the design you can start the cutting.

First drill a small hole well within one of the hearts, then unhitch the coping saw blade from its frame, pass it through the drilled hole, rehitch the blade and fret out the heart. Support the wood on the bench, as illustrated, and work the saw with a good steady, even stroke, trying all the while to keep the angle of cut at about 90° to the face of the wood. Cutting the top cheeks of the hearts is a little tricky because you do have to be careful that you don't knock off the short-grain bridges, so be careful. Finally take the saw from the wood and rub down all the sharp edges of all eight hearts.

Stars within circles

Study the star and circle hex motifs – notice how the five pointed stars are compass drawn and fit the circles. Take the compass and tracing paper, draw a circle with a radius of 1in and then by trial and error, or with a protractor set at 72°, strike off the circumference so that it is divided equally into five. Now link the strike points and draw the characteristic five pointed star. When you are happy that your stars are correct, transfer them to the face-boards, as illustrated.

Note: With a folk carving of this type and character, I think it best if most of the setting out is done by eye. The hex carving is simple enough – clamp the board to be worked on to the bench and then with the $\frac{1}{2}$in flat chisel and the $\frac{1}{2}$in shallow gouge, gently lower the circle, star or segment ground wood. No great depth is needed, so set-in the sides of the stars with the straight chisel and gouge out the ground-wood working from circle edge to cut-in star.

Finishing

When you have worked the hex motifs, the hearts and all the other pierced and shallow carved patterns, go around them with the straight chisel, or a knife, and cut out the little chip-shaped nicks. It's all relatively straight forward, but you will have to take care when you come to the fragile, short-grained wood at the top of the hearts. Just take it a step at a time making sure you don't twist the boards in the clamps or run the gouge into the grain.

Putting together

Look at the photograph and illustrations and see how the face-boards have been dovetailed and set into the side boards.

Draw and mark out the thickness of the side boards on the ends of the face boards and then with the fine toothed saw, cut out the dovetails. Now place the side boards in the vice, front edge uppermost, and using the cut dovetails as patterns, mark, saw and chisel-work the housing – as illustrated. Make sure the dovetail joints are a good tight fit and then fix each of them with a couple of pins. Finally

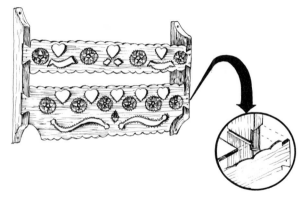

Plate rack and constructional detail. Note how the face board dovetail conceals the housing joints.

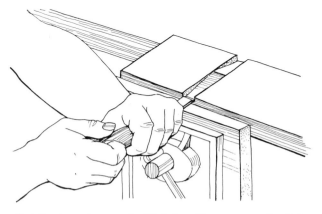

Cut the housing or shelf joints with a saw and a flat chisel.

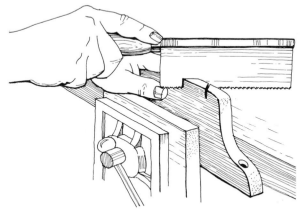

Cut the dovetails with a small saw and shape and work them with a coping saw, rasp and sandpaper.

slide the shelf board into the trench housings and the job is done.

Hints, tips and afterthoughts

The curves at the top and bottom of the end-boards are better worked with a drawknife or spokeshave.

When you rub down with the rasp and sandpaper, don't try and bring the whole thing to a slick finish, just rub off the sharp corners and burrs leaving all the tool marks.

This project needs to look country-made so don't overwork the setting out and carving – it is much better to take the whole thing to a quick finish.

Note: By quick I mean clean, swift and good enough – certainly not shoddy or careless.

Traditionally, little kitchen pieces of this character were painted. Nothing too bright, over shiny or subtle, just good honest earth colours – reds, browns, greens, ochres and the like.

Inspirational design of a front panel from a box dated 1620 which is relief carved and painted red and blue.

Inspirational design of a detail dated 1630.

New England Bible box

In the seventeenth century two English religious separatist groups, the Pilgrims and Puritans, decided to take their faith to America and build a pure and Godly New England. Life for these settlers and pioneers was, without doubt, difficult and hazardous. They quickly had to build shacks and cabins to protect themselves from unfriendly Indians and at the same time they had to battle with an unfamiliar and often hostile environment. The sober and industrious new communities demanded long, tedious days of building, making tools and land clearing. As people settled in they needed basic items of furniture – tables, benches, settles, beds and boxes. There were problems since there were very few craftsmen (most people had only hazy ideas of furniture making and styles), and almost no traditional skills.

Where did they start? With simple hand-made and trade tools, a grindstone, cross-cut saw, drawknife, auger, axe and adze. The settlers went for wood that was closest to hand – Pine, Oak, Birch and Maple. The trees were cut down, rough-sawn or split into boards and generally worked in the raw green state. These wood workers, who had never done it before,

Inspirational design of a detail taken from a chest dated 1675.

Inspirational design of a characteristic New England sunflower design, dated late 1600's.

had neither the time nor the skills to season the wood or bring it to a tooled smooth finish. Furniture of this early American colonial period for reasons of religious purity, shortage of time and lack of skills, tends to be solid, basic and slab-built. As communications with England were almost non-existent, furniture types, motifs, patterns and designs were mostly naïve, village-built improvisations or faint echoes of the simpler English styles. For example, New England furniture of the early eighteenth century still harked back to the English Jacobean, early seventeenth century style and methods of construction: split plank boards, nails and oak pins, wedges and characteristic relief carved strapwork motifs. Of course the remembered European styles and designs varied, as each colony related to its own particular mother-country traditions – English Jacobean, Swedish chip-carved and painted, German, French, Dutch and so on. American colonial furniture of this early period is often referred to as Pilgrim or kitchen hearth and is usually characterized by straight forward construction and shallow relief-carved tulip and sunflower patterns and designs.

Method
Relief carving

Working time
2–3 days

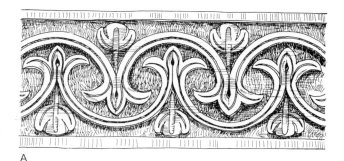

A

B

C

Inspirational designs – **A**. Border design from an English seventeenth-century court cupboard **B**. Jacobean design worked in low relief with incised line details **C**. Elizabethan strapwork motif.

New England Bible box. Seventeenth-century Oak box – the initials R.P. stand for Ruth Plumer who left England in 1634 and went to Massachusetts.

Tools and materials

Traditionally, New England craftsmen were not limited to using a few tried and trusted wood types – if the tree was close at hand and was reasonably straight grained, then it was felled, split, sawn and made into furniture. However the craftsmen, naturally enough, went for the woods that were easy to cut and carve – Pine, Oak, Birch Maple and Cherry. It was common practice to make single items of furniture out of several different wood types, so you might have a Bible box or chest with a softwood Pine base, sides made of a pleasant to carve Oak and a lid of fruitwood. I've chosen to make this project entirely out of 1in thick, straight grained, half seasoned, rough sawn Oak, not only because I feel that it is within the spirit of the colonial period, but it also comes in good widths, ages to a fine rich colour and, best of all, it carves crisply and cleanly.

For tools you will need a small V-section gouge, a small, straight chisel, a wide and shallow, straight gouge, a flat spoon chisel, a small, spoon bit gouge and a shallow curved gouge. And of course you will also need a couple of G-clamps, tracing paper, pencils, measures, mallet, rasp, saws, etc.

Buying and cutting the wood

Visit a supplier and have a good search through his stock – you need four 7in wide boards, two at 30in long, two at 15in and also two slabs 17in wide and 32 in long. When you are looking for suitable wood, don't bother going to the local DIY builders supplier because they usually only stock poor quality prepared softwood timber lengths. It is much better to search out the specialist who is keen to help because he will understand your needs and be prepared to help and advise.

Check your wood over carefully and make sure it is free from shakes, cracks, splits, dead and loose knots, warps and sappy wane-edges.

Setting out the design

When you get your wood home, measure it up and with a square, pencil and saw cut it down so that you have six boards in all – two at 7in × 29in, two at 7in × 15in and two at 16in × 30in as in the working drawings.

Try all through this project to feel yourself into the shoes of a settler who has never done it before. Your tools are limited, you are working in an experimental pioneer environment and you are seeking, to the best of your ability, to make a simple, strong, serviceable and decorative box. Take your wood, board by board, secure it to the bench with the G-clamps and with plane, adze and shallow gouge bring all surfaces to a smooth slightly rippled finish. You aren't after a slick plastic-looking shine, but a soft dappled and gently scalloped tooled texture.

If you look at the photographs and illustrations of the Bible box, you will see that it is quite plain, apart from the single relief-carved front panel. Look thoroughly over the two 29in boards and go for the one which has the straightest grain. With pencil, measure and tracing paper begin to rough out the design, working in your own choice of, say, initials or dates. If you look at the design you will see that although it is more or less symmetrical, the little leaf, stem and flower motifs are individually worked and vary in size, shape and form. Try not to slavishly copy every single cut and stroke, but bring in your own ideas and adjust the designs and motifs as you think fit.

When you are happy with the overall design, pencil press the traced pattern on to the wood, block in the areas that have to be chopped out and then tidy up your work surface and arrange the tools to hand.

Outlining and setting-in the design

With the panel to be carved held firmly with the G-clamps, take up the small V-tool and start to outline the drawn motifs having dapple tooled finish the wood with the adze or gouge. Cut a V-section trench around the whole of your design, all the time working on

Working drawing and detail – the working drawing grid scale is one square to 1in and the detail scale is one and a half squares to 1in. Note the direction of the grain and the simple cut and pinned joints.

The front panel – relief carved design.

the waste or ground side and keeping about $\frac{1}{8}$in away from the drawn lines. As you cut around the design, you will be cutting both across and with the grain of the wood, so always hold the tool with both hands, one guiding and the other pushing and manoeuvring. Work with short, shallow, controlled strokes of the tool and always be ready to brake and stop short if the tool starts to dig too deeply or run away into the grain.

At this stage you won't need to use the mallet, just put your shoulder behind the tool and try to cut a smooth, not too deep, V-trench. Work to a uniform depth of about $\frac{1}{4}$in and be careful when you come to the fragile, thin, short-grain, stalk areas of the motifs. When you have completely outlined the design, you can start to set-in in readiness for clearing, removing or wasting the unwanted ground wood. Hold the small chisel in one hand so that it is upright but leaning slightly over the design, and then work around the motifs with short, sharp, lively taps of the mallet.

Try all the time to keep the depth of cut constant – not to undercut any of the motif edges and to smoothly work the tight angles and turn-arounds. You should be setting-in with a series of quick decisive mallet taps and chisel cuts all the time working to establish a clean, sharp-edged strong design. The chisel needs to cut the wood crisply, especially on the short grain areas, so if you feel the tool crushing rather than cutting, then stop and give it a few strokes on the stone. The setting-in should follow the V-trench and the edge of the design in a single, smooth and continuous line, so if you have a full range of tools, use convex and concave straight gouges when you come to tricky tight curves.

Clamp the wood to the bench and with the adze or gouge take the wood to a dappled, tooled finish.

Once you have drawn in the design, cut-in the drawn lines with a V-tool.

Once the design has been V-trenched you can scoop out the unwanted ground. Note the ground wood can be wasted before or after setting-in.

Clearing or wasting the ground wood

When you have smartly set-in the design with a continuous sharp and crisp cut you can begin to chop and skim out the unwanted ground wood. Take the shallow curve spoon bit chisel and cut a broad trench around the whole of the set-in outline. Once you have established the level or depth of the lowered ground you can clear the whole area. Aim to leave the lowered ground smooth and crisply cut, but not so overworked that you can't see the tool marks. Finally, go around the carving and make sure all the angles between the low ground and raised design are clean and free from bits and pieces, burrs, tears (not tears) and rough edges.

Modelling the raised design

Look carefully at the illustrated Bible box and see how the modelling of the tulips, leaves and flower motifs have been achieved. Notice how the carving is stylized, bold and swift – in fact, just a series of rather mechanical chip-carved nicks and notches.

Take the curved and straight gouges and work the two flower motifs so that they are gently dished and scoop out the wood from side to centre, always taking care that you don't damage the short grained central button. Finally, take the various chisels and gouges and go over the whole design cutting in the various quick crescents, and stylized leaf and flower patterns.

Putting the box together

If you look at the working drawings and details you will see that the box construction is simple and exposed. The ends of the front and back boards are sawn, rebated, lapped over the side boards and then pinned with square nails – there has been no attempt to secret-nail or cover the nails with applied moulding. Before you nail and hinge the box base and lid slabs, go over them with a plane or rasp, shape and dull the edges and give them the distinctive and traditional nosing. Finally, pin a couple of guide battens to the underside of the lid ends and the job is done.

Some carvers prefer to set-in after removing the ground wood and others like to start by setting-in. In this instance I don't think the order of cuts is critical. Try to lower the ground so that it crisply angles up to the raised plateau of the design.

Model the dished flower motifs from side to centre – use a small flat spoon bit gouge and try to work at an angle to the wood grain.

Hints, tips and afterthoughts

The early settlers felled the trees and then split, shaped and carved the wood while it was still green and easily workable. They didn't have the time to wait for the wood to dry out and season. When you are choosing your timber look for wood that has been air drying for about a year and then it won't be too hard and difficult to work.

Old English trestle stool

As far as English furniture is concerned, the Age of Oak is taken to mean the two hundred year period before the Restoration (1660), and it covers such styles as Gothic, Tudor, Elizabethan and Jacobean. What a glorious time it must have been for workers of wood – a country well covered with mature Oak forests and an emerging, prosperous society needing houses, halls and furniture. Of course, the carpenters and carvers used a variety of wood types – Beech, Elm, Chestnut and the like, but generally speaking Oak was so plentiful, cheap, popular and easy to work, that it was the principal building material of the period. The Oaks were cut down in the winter when the sap was low, left in the bark, seasoned and then sawn by a method termed as quartering. Basically, this method of felling, seasoning and converting, results in timber that is beautifully figured and grained and a timber that resists warping and splitting, a perfect wood for the carver.

Although furniture types were pretty basic – for example, tables, chests, cupboards, stools and benches, they were built and carved to a standard that, I believe, has never been bettered. Thick carved slab panels, massive grooved framing, and perfectly fitting mortise and tenon joints all held and clenched with Oak pins and wedges. No nails to rust, no glue to fracture and break down, just square cut Oaken pegs driven through round holes into the joints. Don't think that the houses of the period were jammed full of heavy, dark gloomy lumps of furniture. Far from it. The furniture may have been limited, but when it came to style and decoration, the woodcarvers really let their imaginations run riot. Gothic architecture inspired, tracery motifs were all

Inspirational design of a late fifteenth-century Gothic tracery.

painted and picked out in bright colours; bands of carved foliage were worked around tables, wall panels and beds; there were bulbous, built up and deeply carved table legs; Romanesque portraits were carved on chest fronts and bed heads and much, much more.

The carving of the period has been variously described as being essentially English, robust, youthful and honest. I always think the Age of Oak might better be described as the Age of the woodcarver. However, like all golden ages it just couldn't last. Gradually woodworkers learnt to use thinner timber sections, which in turn forced carvers to scratch about on the surface. Charles, the merry monarch, came back from France and introduced new ideas in furniture and fashion. Suddenly within a ten year period, the vogue was for Walnut, eastern motifs and designs – turned barley sugar legs, marquetry and inlay – the Age of Oak was over.

Method
Pierced and gouge-worked Gothic tracery

Working time
9–10 days

98

Tools and materials

Before you start out on this project look at the photographs and illustrations and then go and visit a few pre-Restoration churches. See how the Gothic tracery has been carved, stepped, cut back into the wood and then pierced. This project isn't for the half-hearted. It's not that you need to be a carving genius because, in fact, the carving stages are relatively simple. It's more that the total bulk and weight of timber, the setting out of the design and the cutting of the joints and carving adds up to a project that is lengthy and extremely hard work.

For a project of this size and character you are going to need a good range of tools and materials – rough work-out paper, large sheets of tracing paper, a measure, a straight edge, a square, pencils, a large compass, a bow saw, a straight saw, a couple of mortise chisels (say a $\frac{1}{2}$in and 1in), a hand drill, a spokeshave or small drawknife, a selection of gouges, rasps and rifflers, a couple of G-clamps and, of course, the use of a good solid work bench. For timber, you need 2in thick slabs of smooth-sawn oak – two pieces 14in wide and 24in long, one piece 12in wide and 24in long and one piece 6in wide and 24in long. When you are buying the wood, look for material that is quarter sawn. It will probably be more expensive, but for wide-board work it will pay you to get the best and then you won't have to worry about excessive warping and shrinking. Look closely at the boards and make sure that they are free from split end, sapwood edges, dead knots and extreme grain twists.

Setting out the design

When you get your timber home, check it again and then with measure, square and saw set it out and cut it to size. Now look at the gridded working drawings and see how the two end-boards or uprights are identical and symmetrical. Take the boards and with the aid of rough paper and square tracing paper, set out the curved profiles, the position of the carved tracery roundels, the cross-rail mortises, the seat tenons, etc. It's a good idea at

An old English trestle or bench stool made from Oak, with pierced and carved tracery.

this stage to draw up centre lines on the wood, work half the motifs and curves and then trace and transfer the design to fit. Work the cross-rail board in the same way – cut it to size and then set out the position of the pierced tracery design, the shoulders of the tenons and the clamp-wedge mortises. When all the setting out is complete, pin your working drawings around the workshop, clean-up and arrange your tools so that they are comfortably to hand.

Working the trestle ends

When the lines of the traced design have been pencil press transferred to the working face of the timber thicken them up and then clearly label or block-in the areas that have to be left, cut or pierced. Clamp the trestle ends, one by one, in the vice and cut the profiles with the bow saw as illustrated. Don't worry about technique, as long as you cut on the waste side of the design and not twist, buckle or break the saw blade you shouldn't have any problems. Saw with a good steady stroke, all the time manoeuvring the blade around the curves,

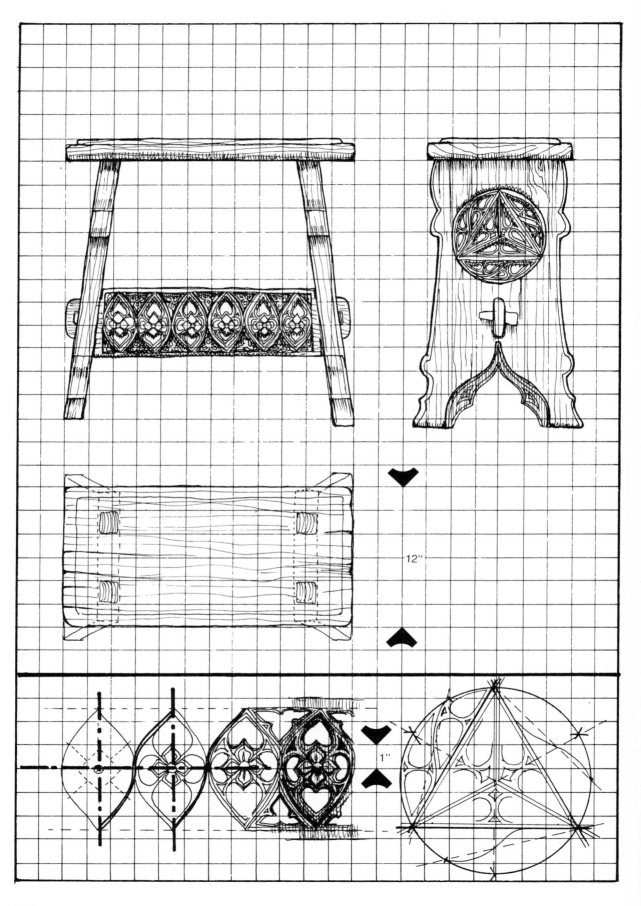

12"

1"

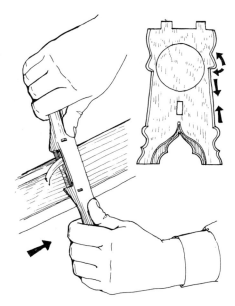

When you have drawn out the design on the end boards, cut the profiles with a bow saw and work the curves with a spokeshave. Note the various directions of cut.

Establish the roundel tracery design and then drill saw-blade guide holes.

speeding up the stroke at tight corners and keeping the blade square with the working surface of the wood.

When both end-boards have been sawn, set them in the vice, one at a time, and smooth the various curves with either a wooden or metal flat-faced spokeshave. Work from side to centre on the concave profiles and you will then be able to achieve a good smooth cut without chopping into or splitting the grain. With the convex curves do the opposite working the spokeshave from top to side or hill to valley.

Once all the curves have been sawn and smoothed take the spokeshave and bevel or chamfer the sharp edges using swift cuts that take off the corners of the wood.

Measuring, marking out and carving the tracery roundels

Place the end-boards square on the work surface and with the compass and measure set

Working drawing and tracery detail – the working drawing grid scale is six squares to 12in and the detail is one square to 1in. Note the hole and wedge joint, the mortise and tenon seat joints and the compass drawn tracery.

out the tracery. Set the compass to a radius of 4in and then, working to the centre line as illustrated, draw in the circles. With the compass still fixed at the same radius and starting at the top of the circle, go around the circumference striking off arcs – six in all. Link them with straight lines, as illustrated, and then draw in the triangles, segments and tracery. Use tracing paper to get the single motifs just right and pencil press transfer and build up the rest of the design to fit.

Carving the tracery roundels

If you study the various illustrated pierced tracery motifs you will see that they are all made up of geometrically drawn designs, carved and worked so that there are bands of high relief and stepped horizontal, vertical and hollow mouldings. The carved steps cut into and pierce the wood – the thicker the wood the more steps. Establish the position of the windows and then label the areas *leave, lower, hollow out, angle* and *pierce*.

Decide just how intricate you want the tracery to be – the number of steps and

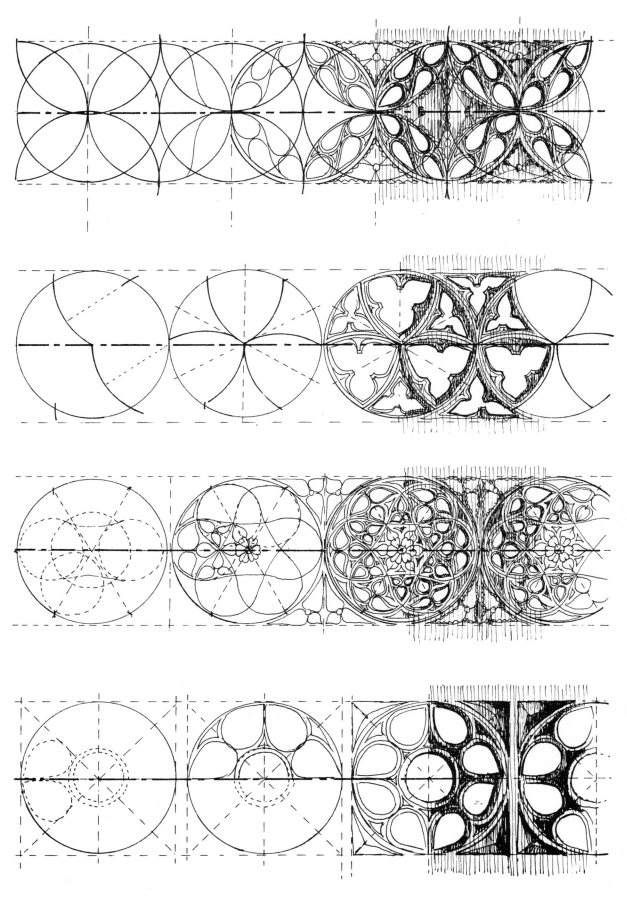

hollows – and then take the drill and pierce the waste ground. Now take the coping, pad, keyhole or fine bow saw and with the wood clamped in the vice cut away the little windows. See how the tracery is very much like deep-relief work, the only difference being the stylized moulding and the pierced ground.

If you study church window traceries you will see that the designs relate directly to the weight of masonry pushing down on the window arch and the need for the weight to be spread and directed throughout the structure. Consequently the amount of stone used tends to be large, with a great many intricate steps, feathers and mouldings. The furniture carver has no such problems since he can reduce the thickness of wood, simplify the curves, cut out tracery bars, exaggerate the cusps (little triangular fill-ins or projected points between two curves), or anything else that takes his fancy.

Once you have sketched in the width of the steps and hollow faces on the working surface of the wood you can start the carving. Take a shallow curve, straight gouge and lower the first step which should take you down into the wood by $\frac{1}{4}$in. Next, take the shallow curve, spoon chisel and work the hollow curve of the face mould. It all sounds most complicated, but in fact all you are doing is cutting down into the wood in a series of steps and hollows. Once you have carved the moulding and the linked cusps, you can chop out the little triangular fillet within the cusp rather like chip carving.

Note: It's not a bad idea to gouge away, dish and reduce the thickness of wood at the back of the roundel (see photograph) – it makes for easy drilling and sawing.

Finally, when you have carved and worked the roundel and cleaned up the tight angles of the piercing, take a shallow curve gouge and go over the wood giving it a very light, tooled finish.

Inspirational designs of various tracery designs showing the compass drawn grids. Note how most of the motifs are based on a six or eight division of the circle.

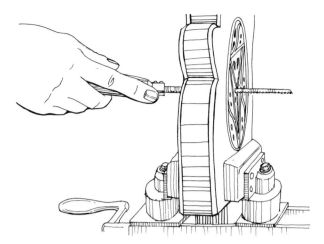

With a coping, pad or key-hole saw, cut and work the tracery windows. Note that if you find the going difficult, reduce the thickness of wood by dishing the back roundel with a gouge as in the photograph.

Once you have pierced and cut the tracery holes, lower the ground by $\frac{1}{4}$in and then work the curve of the face-mould with a spoon bit gouge.

Carving and piercing the cross-rail

Take up the piece of 6in × 24in timber, place it squarely on the work surface and have at hand the tracing paper and compass. If you have a good look at the illustrated cross-rail carving you will see that there are six motifs in all. If you now analyze the total design you will see that it is made up of overlapping 3in circles, with the overlaps and cusps being pierced,

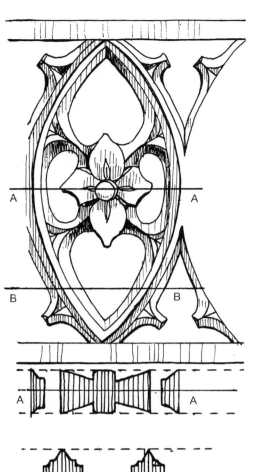

Details of the carved cross-rail. The tracery is cut and worked like the roundel – the design is drawn up, the tracery is drilled and sawn and the steps of the moulding are worked with a spoon bit gouge.

bossed and carved. Carve as with the roundel – that is, you accurately draw up the design, the widths of the steps and hollows and then you set to with the drill, coping saw and gouges as illustrated.

Putting together

Take the four timbers, the two uprights, the seat-board and the cross-rail, and with the square, bow saw, straight saw, mortise chisel and mallet cut and work all the joints. First set out, angle and cut the four mortises on the seat-board and then cut the end-board tenons, the two cross-rail mortises, the cross-rail tenons and finally the clamp-wedge mortises on the ends of the cross-rail. Along the way, check and double check your measurements, making sure that all the angles and tenon

shoulders are correct. Now cut the wedge slots in the four seat tenons, knock in hardwood wedges and rub them down flush with the seat-board. Finally, make a couple of cross-rail clamping wedges out of some off-cuts and bang them home.

Hints tips and afterthoughts

When the job is done, the Oak can be rubbed down and darkened with linseed oil, left to dry and then polished with beeswax.

Note: If you want the oil to dry quickly, add a drop of turpentine – 1 part turpentine to 3 parts oil.

You might want to change the order of working. You could cut all the joints, put the stool together, check the fit, knock it apart and then do the carving.

Built-up Work

Pied Piper of Hamlin

Delicate miniature figures of this size and character are typical of Black Forest wood-carving. The Black Forest in southern Germany is big, about a hundred miles long and forty miles wide. It is a place of deep, dark, lonely conifer woods, small hill-cupped lakes and gothic horror legends. When I think of the Black Forest, I imagine a whole mish-mash of fairy-tale figures and folk craft traditions. Little Red Riding Hood, wolves and wood cutters, Snow White and mysterious forest glades, the Pied Piper of Hamlin, dream-like castles, cottagers making puppets that come to life, medieval clock figures and much, much more.

However, legend and the brothers Grimm apart, the whole region is in reality a wood carver's paradise, with lonely rural craftsmen carving everything from simple kitchen ware, to wooden dolls, string-puppets, altar figures and cuckoo clocks. I would say that the Black Forest and neighbouring Bavaria are unique in Europe in that not only do they still have a wood carving tradition, but the tradition is living, growing and flourishing. For example in Oberammergau, the village famous for its Passion plays, most of the villagers are wood carvers, the main source of income is wood carving and, better still, there is a wood carving school.

Traditional Black Forest carvings are characterized by being worked in close-grained Lime and Box wood, by being figurative and by being painted. Realistic intricately carved folk and fairy-tale miniature figures, all having beautifully worked, twisted and fluttering draperies and all perfectly considered poses.

Method
Gouge and knife-work in the round

Working time
5–10 days

Pied Piper of Hamlin. Early twentieth-century, German, carved in Lime and painted.

Tools and materials
For this project you need to use a wood that is hard, fine, knot-free and smooth grained. Make your first choice English or European Box, but failing that you could make-do with, say, top quality Lime or Holly. Look for a piece of wood that is about 4in wide, 3in thick and 9in long. Bear in mind that Box wood only

Inspirational designs. When you are working a carving of this type and character it is helpful to make a sketchbook of ideas and details.

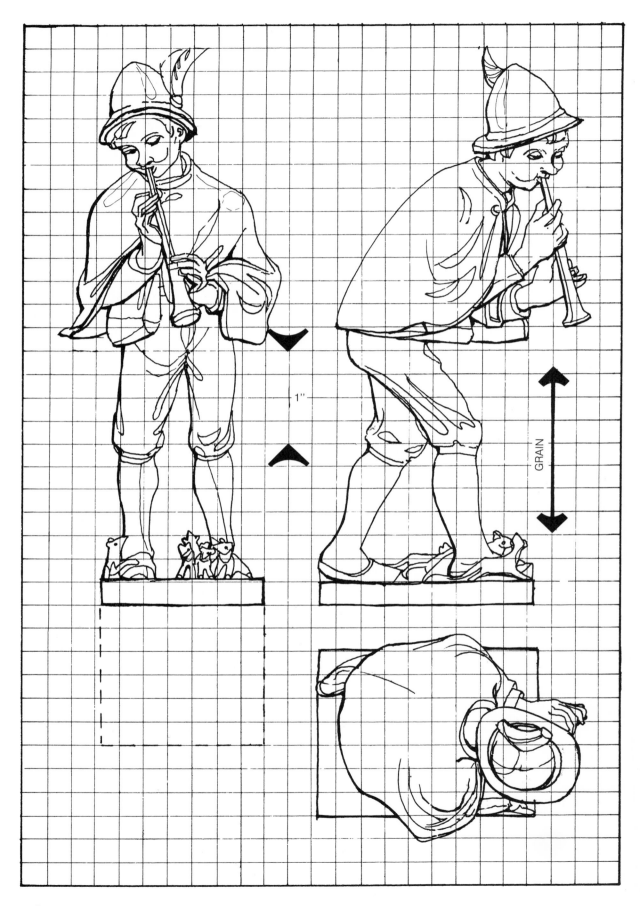

1"

GRAIN

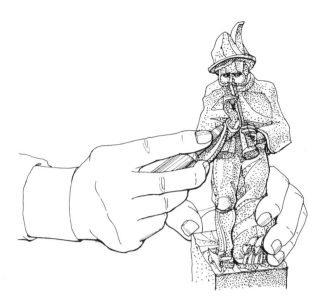

Start by making a plastercine maquette.

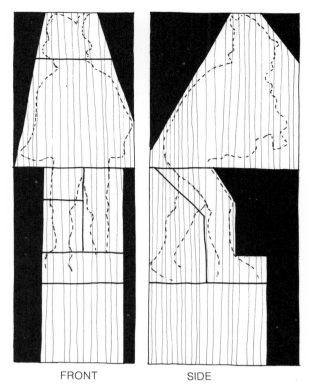

FRONT   SIDE

When you have decided how the figure should look, draw the design on the wood and then cut away the waste wood with a coping saw.

comes in relatively small pieces, and these tend to have end splits and stains, so choose your wood with great care, and certainly avoid pieces that have twists, dead knots and look to be unseasoned.

For tools, you need the full range of a coping saw, a pad saw, a hand drill, a set of rifflers, a good selection of small-curve straight, bent and spoon bit gouges, a couple of knives, a penknife and a scalpel, plastercine, pencils and paper. And, of course, the use of a bench and vice, or a really solid kitchen-type table and a pair of carver's chops.

Setting out the design – making a plastercine maquette

Look closely at the drawings and photographs for this project, decide how you want the figure to be and then collect helpful magazine pictures of figure, hand, face and feet details. Now take the plastercine and build a full size working model or maquette.

Consider how the legs and arms of the figure fit and work in relationship to each other and the total pose, then model the plastercine

Working drawing – the grid scale is four squares to 1in. Note the direction of the grain and the pierced areas in and around the pipe and hands.

accordingly. With this project, the tricky bit is the cutting and carving of the small areas in and around the chin, pipe and hands so, at the outset, consider carefully just how complex you want your carving to be and then adjust the design to fit. For example, do you want the hands and arms extended? Or would you prefer a more tight pose? Perhaps you want a carving with the legs together or with the legs as part of the main body of wood? Or maybe you want to re-shape the whole pose and have the figure sitting? These are all points to sort out at the beginning of the project when you are setting up the plastercine maquette. When the model is finished, put it within reach but out of harm's way and then arrange the tools comfortably to hand.

Marking out and first cuts

With pencil and paper draw out front and side views of the figure and then pencil press transfer your drawings to the working faces of your piece of wood. Thicken up the main

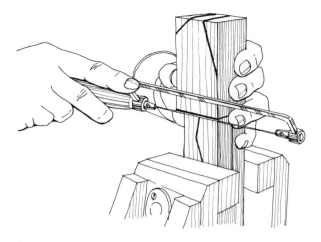

When you are using the coping saw, support the wood in the vice, work with a steady and even action and be careful that you don't twist the blade.

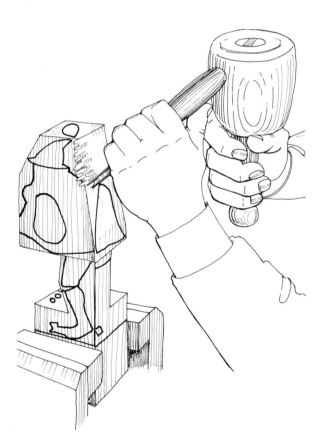

With a small gouge and mallet, round and model all the rough-sawn corners and edges as you work. You will consequently have to continually re-establish the design.

profile lines and then clearly label the wood *top, side, back, waste* and so on. If at this stage you still have doubts as to just how the figure is

to be worked, or the order of work, then look again at the drawings, maybe actually make a plastercine block and have, as it were, a trial run. It is vital, before you start working on the wood for real, that you have a crystal-clear picture in your mind of just how the figure is to emerge from the wood.

Cutting away the waste

Put your block of wood in the vice so that you can see it front side on and then with the drill, pad saw and coping saw, cut away the waste. Clear the wood at either side of the head, below the level of the cloak and between the legs. Work with care and be mean with the amount of wood that you chop out. Once this is done, re-position the block so that it is side view on, and cut away the waste above the shoulders, the small bits in and around the hands, chin and chest and the wedge between the legs. Work with caution, don't be hasty, and keep on referring to the drawings, magazine clips and model. When you have cut out the blank, take the pencil and re-establish the main lines of the form and cross hatch in the areas that need to be worked.

Modelling the form

With the wood still in the vice or bench chops, as illustrated, take a small straight gouge and start to round-up all the rough-sawn corners and edges. Don't try to complete single areas but go over the whole figure cutting away the wood searching out the main shapes and forms.

As you work, try and think of the finished carving as being a figure that is hidden away in the body of wood. With this in mind, don't attempt to rip off all the concealing layers of wood in one great gouge thrust, but gently pare away until you feel that the lines of the form are revealed. Work with the whole range of tools, using the one that you consider best for the present job, and establish the curve of the shoulders, the bulge and tension of the calf muscles and the humped roundness of the head and back. As you work always keep your tools razor-sharp and be constantly aware of the changing direction of the wood grain.

Final cuts

Work the figure from the head, face and hands down to the trousers, knees and shoes and gradually bring the carving to completion. Constantly turn the wood in the vice, walk around your work, refer to the drawings and model, stand back be very critical. Along the way carve and work the wood with a feather-light touch, finally taking a fine-blade scalpel and one of the small rifflers to cut and work the details of the face and hands.

Finishing

You will get to a point when you have to decide just how far you want the carving to be finished. For example do you want the face to be smooth and perfect in every detail? Are you going to try and show every last fingernail and eyelash? Do you want the marks of the tools to show? My Pied Piper, as illustrated, has a smooth-to-the-touch cape, hat, drapes and legs, but otherwise the face and hands have been quite roughly tooled. So take the finish as far as you feel it ought to go, then work the whole carving with the scalpel and tidy up all the cuts, nooks and crannies.

Painting

Put away all your cutting tools, brush down your work area, and place the carving square on the work bench. Mix up several thin colour washes and then with a soft hair brush, give the whole carving just a hint of colour. A slight suggestion of grey on the trousers, a delicate touch of orange for the cape, a touch of green for the cap, and pick out the eyes and buttons with brown. Finally, when the wood is dry, swiftly rub down the carving with the finest flour paper and give it a coat or two of clear beeswax.

Hints, tips and afterthoughts

This carving is tricky, and there's no single and easy way of working. All I can say is – choose the best wood, keep your tools sharp,

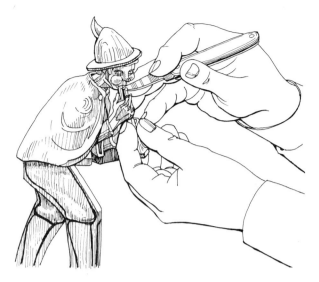

When you carve the delicate pipe and hand details support the wood with one hand and guide your knife with the other.

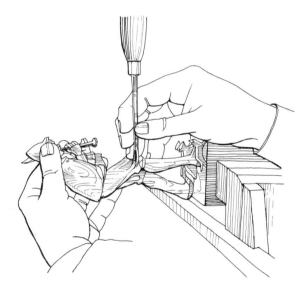

Finally, cut-in the drape folds with a small spoon bit gouge.

don't be in a rush and keep referring to your drawings.

You will have to be extra careful when you come to the short-grain upturned edge of the cloak. Use a spoon bit gouge, work across the grain and don't twist or jar the tool. If you happen to split or damage part or all of the figure, don't despair, make repairs with PVA glue, leave it to dry for twenty four hours and then continue working.

Inspirational design of a detail from another Grinling Gibbons carving. Note the Gibbons pea pod trade mark.

Grinling Gibbons flower

Grinling Gibbons was born in Rotterdam, Holland, in the year 1648. His background is a little misty, but it is thought that his father was English and his mother Dutch. It's not on record exactly when and why he came to England, all we know for sure is that when he was a young man he was discovered by the author, diarist and man of letters, John Evelyn. Evelyn says of his meeting with Gibbons, 'He was working in an obscure place . . . a poor solitary cottage.' Fortunately for Gibbons, Evelyn was more than just interested in art and sculpture, he was the author of *Sylva*, a book about forest trees and timber usage, and he was also an active and influential member of the Royal Society.

Grinling Gibbons carving with characteristic flowers, pea pods and delicate undercutting.

Gibbons's wood carvings must have made a big impression on Evelyn, because within the month they had been seen by Sir Christopher Wren the architect, Samuel Pepys the naval official and diarist and Charles II. No doubt Gibbons was soon overwhelmed with work and commissions – statuary for the King, swags and flowers for the Queen, carvings for Wren's great buildings, mirror frames, over-mantles, coats of arms, gifts for foreign ambassadors, cherubs, swags and much, much more. The Gibbons' style of woodcarving was taken up by most of the important architects of the period and worked into their decorative schemes. Birds, angels, cupids, flowers, shells, ribbons and swags, all worked in Lime wood and carved in a style that has variously been described as naturalistic, florid and exuberantly realistic.

Although Gibbons died in 1720, his work set the style for the next hundred years – birds, flowers and animals, all worked realistically; the Lime wood being built-up, laminated, glued, pinned and deeply undercut.

Working drawings – the grid scale is four squares to 1in. Note the direction of the grain.

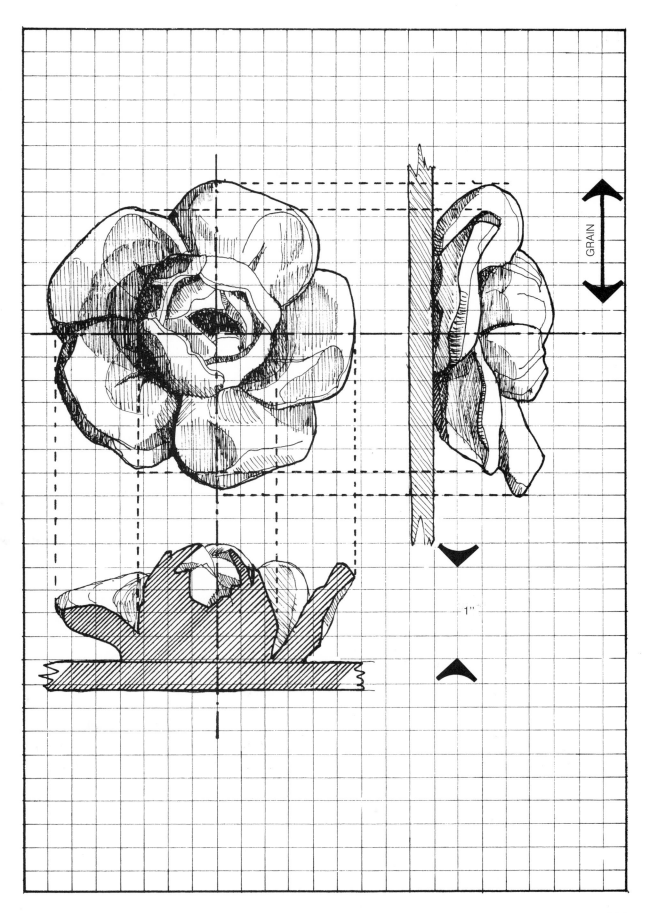

GRAIN

1"

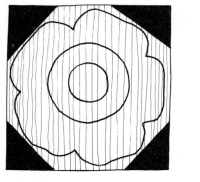

Draw the design out on the wood and block in the areas that need to be cut away.

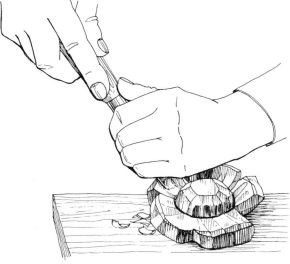

When you have cut away the unwanted wood with a coping saw, take a shallow straight gouge, lower the wood round the flower centre and generally shape-up the petal profile.

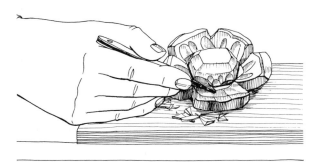

Take a fine blade knife or a small chisel, and undercut the central ball of the flower.

Method
Carving in the round and undercutting

Working time
1–2 days

Tools and materials
For this project you must use Lime. It has little grain, very few knots and best of all it can be cut and worked in just about any direction. Get yourself a small block of wood of 4in × 4in and $1\frac{1}{2}$–2in thick as illustrated in the working drawings. For tools, you will need a couple of small spoon bit gouges, a shallow curved gouge, a small, shallow curved, straight gouge, a flat spoon bit gouge, a small knife and, of course, a bench stop or clamp and such items as a pencil, sketch paper, measure, coping saw and rifflers.

Before you start this project take a good look at the photographs and working drawings and consider how the flower fits the wood and the grain.

Setting out the design
Take up your block of wood, check it over thoroughly and make absolutely sure that it is free from soft, waney wood, splits, grain twists and orange/brown pulpy knots. Start by tracing the various views of the flower and transferring them to the top, bottom and sides of the block. If you look at the photograph and the working drawings you will see that I have simplified, further stylized and slightly thickened the flower petals.

If, for instance, you want to add more petals or have a more complex flower centre then this is the time to re-adjust your sketches.

When you have drawn in the various elevations of the flower, block them in with a pencil and make clear notes on the wood – *top, side A, cut away* and so on.

First cuts
Take the coping saw and clear away all the unwanted wood and establish the basic flower profile. When this has been done you will find that the little block of wood is awkward to hold and difficult to manage, so glue it to a larger piece of thick plywood which makes for easy holding and clamping. If you decide to screw the Lime to the ply, rather than glue, be careful that the screws don't split the wood or pierce areas that are to be carved as illustrated.

Shaping up

Clamp the plywood-supported, roughed-out, block of wood to the work bench and then start chopping in with a small, shallow curve, straight gouge. Hold the gouge in both hands and work around the flower plan, all the time cutting straight down into the wood. When you are carving, don't lever against the wood but cut away small crisp curls and gradually work closer and closer to the outside edge of the plan view of the flower. When this is done, take the small straight chisel and cut a V-trench around the central ball of the flower.

Once you have set-in around the flower centre, take a small spoon bit gouge and working from the flower edge to the centre cut away, slope and lower the ground. Continue carving in this way cutting in and around the central area and then gouging out and lowering the petal ground. When the centre pillar of wood stands well proud of the lowered petals, it can be rounded and undercut.

Model the petals with a small spoon bit gouge carving from side to centre.

Final cuts

Take up the small spoon bit gouge and start to hollow out the centre of the flower. Work as if you were spooning into a boiled egg. That is, you push the spoon bit gouge deep into the centre of the flower and then scoop out a curl of wood. It does sound rather complicated, but in fact, as long as you keep your tools sharp and don't rush or be tempted to lever your tools, then this project is really quite straight forward. Once you have hollowed out the flower centre, take the shallow curved, curved gouge, and cleanly work and tool the top surface of the out-spread petals. See how the petals appear to overlap each other and gently curve and ripple at their edges.

When you have established and tooled the top surface of the petals and the flower centre, take one of the spoon bit gouges and start to undercut the petals. Work with a light sensitive touch and only attempt to remove small parings of wood – don't lever up against the now fragile petals or try to hack off great chunks of wood.

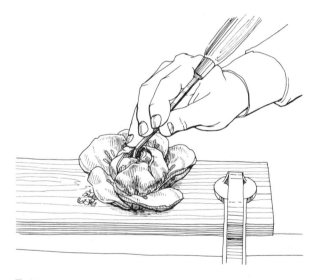

Take a small spoon bit gouge and spoon out the flower centre as if you were digging into a hard boiled egg. Work little by little and be careful that you don't break off any delicate short-grain.

The finished flower.

Finishing

Stand back from your work and try to see it with a fresh and critical eye. Can you work the petals thinner? Are the petal overlaps convincing? Search out and correct faults and when you feel that enough is enough, take the small knife and riffler and go over the whole flower working a delicate, tooled finish. Slide the razor-sharp knife over the wood and pare away any rough areas, clean up the undercuts and finally cut-in the little stylized petal creases.

Hints, tips and afterthoughts

With a rather delicate carving of this character, there are several tricky areas of short-grain. For example, the tips of the petals and the fine edge of the flower centre have to be worked and carved with extra care.

If you find that your tools are cutting-up roughly and leaving a ragged finish, then spend a few minutes honing them to a keen edge on the oilstone and leather strop.

If in the final stages of carving you split a petal, don't lose your temper. Check that the break is clean and then mend it with a PVA wood glue or an epoxy resin. Bind up the mend with fine cotton, leave it for twenty four hours, and then go back to work.

Victorian counterbalance horse

Charles Dickens, Christmas trees, lamplit rooms, blazing fires, ghost stories, top hats, toys and steamships – the word Victorian brings all these to mind. But for me the most vivid of these rather sentimental images is that of a firelit room full of toys and children. The Victorians had a passion for toys – big, marvellous, craftsman built, engines of delight. Toys made of varnished and painted woods, gleaming brass and bright painted tin-plate. Not for Victorian children a heap of electronic chip-controlled throwaway plastic. They had huge, brassbound steam engines that actually hissed and chugged around playroom

Inspirational design of a Victorian toy horse and cart, carved and painted.

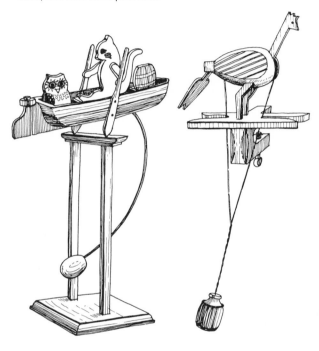

Inspirational designs. Victorian balancing toys come in many shapes and sizes. On the left is The Owl and The Pussy Cat – see how the boat rocks on the oars. On the right is a pendulum toy called The Nodding Ostrich – as the weight swings the tail and head nods.

floors, sultry slant-eyed French dolls, carved and painted rocking horses, carved Nuremberg dolls, Noah's arks with carved and painted animals, dolls houses, marionettes and brightly painted toy soldiers.

Of all Victorian toys, my favourite is a beautiful little carved and painted balancing horse that stands on a sort of flagpole arrangement. He seems to defy gravity – he can rock on a pin-head or even on a single strand of stretched thread. Carved and painted working toys of this character were made, more often than not, in Germany in the nineteenth century. They didn't have motors, springs,

Carved and painted horse (made by the author). Note the stylized painted designs and the counter-balance wire.

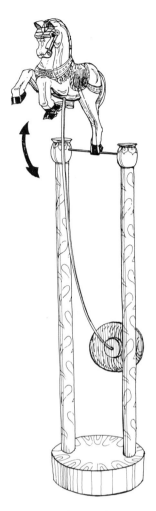

The finished counterbalance horse on a stand. Note how the counterbalance action enables the horse to balance on a single hoof.

magnets or anything complicated but were operated by simple balance and counter-balance weights.

Toys of the counterbalance type come in a great many shapes and sizes – little ducks that bob and peck, nursery rhyme animals in rocking boats, horses with and without riders, juggling clowns and dancing ladies. Sometimes the characters are made of little lathe turned bits and bobs – arms, legs and wooden ball heads, and sometimes they are flat and stylized. But nearly always they are worked in wood, beautifully made, nicely carved and brightly painted and decorated.

Method
Built-up and carved in the round

Working time
2–3 days

Tools and materials
One of the pleasures of working a project of this type is that you can adjust the working methods, designs and materials to suit your own needs. If, say, you admire the New Forest art and craft toymakers, you might want to carve a horse to scale and paint it naturalistic-ally; on the other hand, if American colonial primitive woodcarving is your passion, per-haps you would want to make the horse flat with a minimum of carving and then paint it with basic earth colours. I've chosen to work this toy in what might be described as the English Victorian, fairground rocking horse style – the horse is carved in the round with exaggerated features and then painted and patterned with brilliant primary colours.

For this project you need a good range of tools and materials – a coping saw, a small

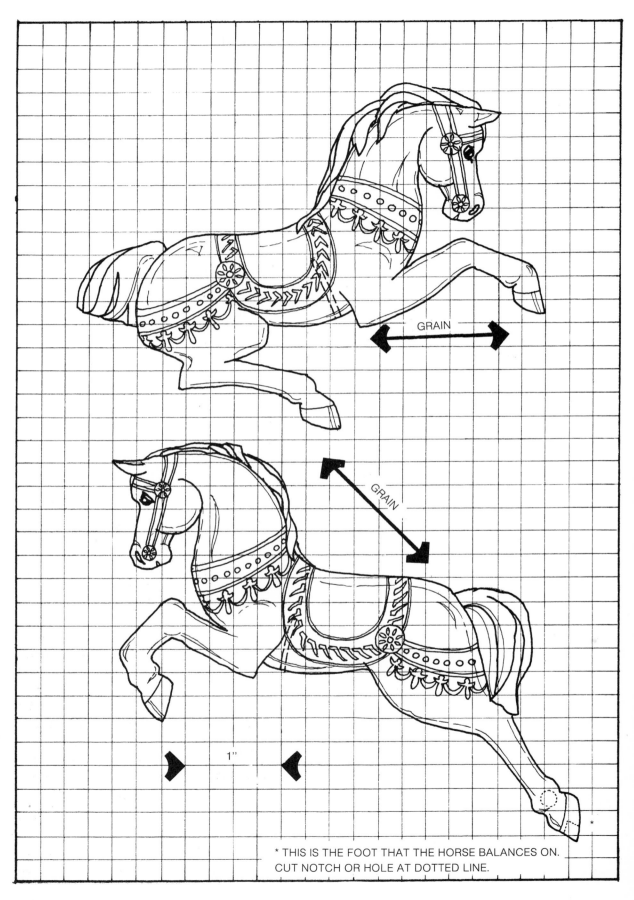

GRAIN

GRAIN

1"

* THIS IS THE FOOT THAT THE HORSE BALANCES ON.
CUT NOTCH OR HOLE AT DOTTED LINE.

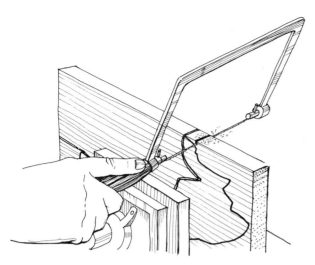

Draw out the horse's profile and cut out with a fine blade coping saw.

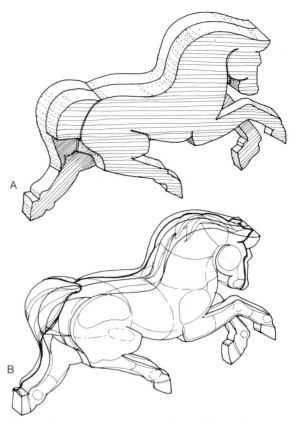

Check that the two cut-outs fit. **A**. Carve the inside legs, glue the two halves together and then cut, carve and work the total horse form **B**. Cutting lines to help shape the horse.

straight gouge, a small curved gouge, a small flat spoon bit gouge, a knife, a rasp and rifflers, PVA wood glue or resin glue, a vice or clamp, plenty of sketch and tracing paper, a selection of fine-grade model makers paints and pencils, measure, turpentine, fine brushes and the like. For wood, you need two pieces of 1in thick, 6in × 6in prepared Lime as in the working drawing. As always, when you are buying wood, spend a long time looking over it and in this case make sure it's clean, a good cream colour, and free from knots, twists and splits.

Setting out the design
Take a good look at the working drawings and see how the horse has been sawn, built-up and then worked. Start by drawing up the design, reworking the horse profiles, enlarging or whatever else you feel needs altering and then trace and pencil press transfer the horse patterns on to the working faces of your two pieces of wood. Check that the grain is running from nose to tail, mark in the areas that have to be cut away and you are then ready for the off.

Working drawing – the grid scale is four squares to 1in. Note how the horse is worked in two halves and that each half needs to be worked with a different grain direction. Keep the design chunky with the minimum of weak short-grain areas. The rear hoof can be drilled for a wire or notched.

Take up the coping saw, secure the wood in the vice and carefully cut out the two profiles. When you are sawing, keep the blade at 90° to the working face of the wood and only cut on the waste side of the drawn design. See how the two cut-out profiles come together, head to head and body to body, and how the four legs are off-set. When you are happy with the overall shape of the horse profiles label them *working face*, *glue face*, *inside leg* and so on. Before you go any further, hold the two cut-outs glue face to glue face, and make sure that they are a good and flush fit.

Carving the inside legs
Take up the profiles, one by one, clamp them to your bench so that the glue sides are face up and then start to carve and model the inside leg areas. With the small straight gouge, cut off the sharp edges and reduce the wood thickness by about a third. Don't try to achieve a

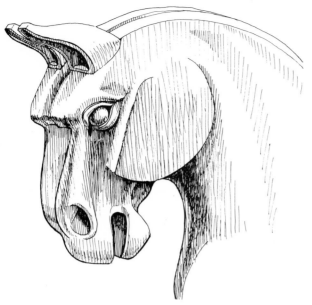

Inspirational design of a nineteenth century, carousel horse detail. Note the exaggerated cheeks.

Inspirational design of a traditional and characteristic merry-go-round horse.

realistically fully carved hoof and fetlock, just round the wood so that the various shapes are smooth and sculptural. Do this with all four legs.

From time to time, fit the two halves of the horse together, see if the curves of the legs look right, and then check on the distance between the legs. By the time you have rounded the legs and reduced the wood thickness there

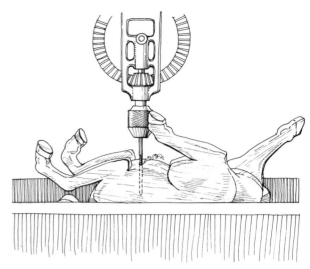

Once you have carved and modelled the horse, support it upside-down in a padded vice and drill the hole for the counterbalance wire.

should be a nice feeling of leg movement and a suggestion of the chest and upper leg muscle.

Glueing, building up and marking out
Hold the two horse profiles together and check that the glue sides fit smooth and flush. Now spread PVA or resin glue on the glue sides, bring them together and put them in the clamp. When the glue is dry, take the horse from the clamp and compare it with your inspirational drawings, photographs and working drawings. At this point, before you go any further, pencil in the main forms and indicate whether or not they have to be for instance, left, lowered or rounded.

Modelling and rounding the form
Start by putting the horse in the vice and arranging the saw and the various gouges comfortably to hand. Take the saw and make a $\frac{1}{4}$in deep stop–cut just above the line of the shoulder. With one of the small flat gouges, and working across the grain from the top of the head to the shoulder, chop into the stop-cut and lower the wood by about $\frac{1}{4}$in. The horse shape should now be more or less roughed out and ready for carving.

With the small gouge chop out the shape of the horse's back, belly and neck and generally go over the form establishing the main roundnesses. As the horse's head is the main focus of attention and also relatively difficult to carve, decide just how the eyes, nostrils, nose, etc. are going to be cut on a few extra sketch-pad and plastercine work-outs. Once again, don't try to carve a realistic horse, it is much better to concentrate on the main expressive features and enlarge and exaggerate the forms. Gouge, hollow and flare the nostrils, cut the shape of the eyes, shape the ears, round the cheeks, cut in the mouth and teeth, and carve the tail and mane. Continue to work keeping the tools moving across and around the grain, and referring to the working drawings and inspirational pictures. Carving the legs is a little bit tricky because in places they are short-grained, so use a knife and riffler and be very careful not to twist or wrench the tools. Finally, with the knife and the small flat spoon bit gouge, go over the whole horse cutting in the harness, decoration and saddle as illustrated.

Finishing

When you think that the carving is finished, stand back and look at it critically. Could the legs be a shade thinner? Should the teeth nash and the nostrils flare? Has the tail and mane got enough swish? When you are sure that the project has gone as far as it's going, take the rifflers and the graded sandpapers, and bring the wood to a smooth-to-the-touch finish. Finally, drill a hole in the belly of the horse and make the counterbalance support out of coathanger wire. Carve a weight out of a piece of hardwood and fix the wire to the horse's body, as illustrated.

Painting

It is important when you are painting that the whole work area is free from shavings and dust, so clean-up and put away your carving tools first. Clamp the counterbalance wire in the vice and arrange the horse so that he is at a good working height. Now's the time to sit back and decide on colours – are you going to have a black and white dappled finish in the Victorian rocking horse tradition? Or are you going for brilliant colours – golds, reds and

When painting the horse, give it several coats of primer, two undercoats and a gloss coat and pick out the hooves, eyes and mouth with black paint. Note that for a super smooth finish, rub down between coats.

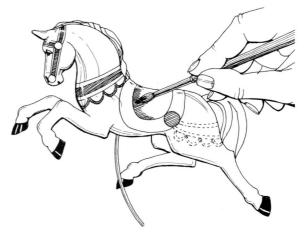

Paint the harness and trappings with bright primary colours and gold. Don't try for subtle realism, but go for bold designs and motifs.

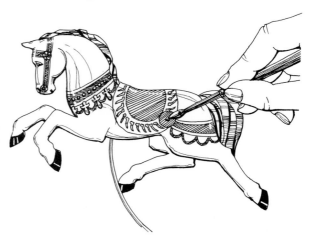

When you paint the gold take care that it doesn't bleed into the other colours.

I used a wooden ball for the counterbalance, but as it was too light I had to drill it and weight it with lead shot.

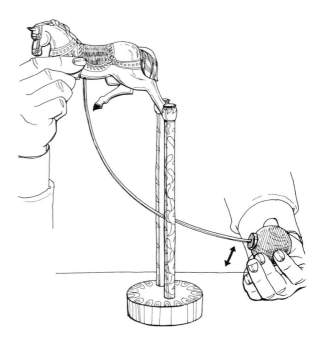

The final fixing is a little tricky. Bend, shape and shorten the wire until the horse maintains a prancing balance by trial and error.

blues, like Victorian fairground horses? Choose your colours, sketch out your designs and patterns and then arrange your painting materials comfortably to hand.

First give the whole horse three or four thick primer coats, rubbing down between coats and then finish with two undercoats and a single top coat. When you come to painting the details such as the eyes, mouths, harness patterns etc, use a very fine sable brush and high gloss, find grade, model maker's paints. Don't try and paint realistic subtle colours since it is much better to have, say, a white or primary red ground, and then pick out the details with gold, blue, black and toned primaries, as illustrated.

Final points

The weight of the counterbalance and the curve of the wire will be dictated by the precise weight of the finished horse. If you find that the carved counterbalance bob needs to be heavier, drill it, add some lead shot, plug the hole with a filler and then paint it to suit.

This toy will balance on a shelf edge, the edge of a table, a taught cord line or even the point of a needle. If you want a set display piece, you can make a stand, as illustrated.

Hints, tips and afterthoughts

When you are painting, the brush strokes need to be bold, simple and direct – plenty of sweeping curves and both thick and thin lines.

When you are carving the body watch out that you don't crush the short-grain legs in the vice. You could always put anti crush blocks between the horse's legs to prevent this happening.

Useful Information

Glossary of tools

Adze A cutting tool that has an arched blade at right angles to the handle. In use it is swung like a pendulum with the heavy cutting edge removing scoops of wood.

Auger A tool rather like a brace and bit used to cut and drill holes.

Axe A small wood carver's axe can be used for the initial wood preparation. For example, if you are cleaning up a piece of found wood, you might remove all the bark and branch spurs with an axe.

Bent or curved tools Back bent tools are very much like spoon bit tools in that they have a wood-scooping bowl at the blade end.

Bench A wood carver's bench might be four-square and purpose made like a carpenter's bench – chest high and used for miniatures, or just a large strong, kitchen cottage type, table. All that is required of a good carver's bench is that it is strong, stable and solid enough to take a variety of clamps, vices and holdfasts.

Bent tools These come in many shapes and sizes. They have the same cutting sections as straight gouges and chisels, the only difference being that the shafts of the tools are curved backwards so that they can be used for carving recesses, inside bowl curves and the like.

Bow saw A thin bladed saw set in a wooden frame used for cutting curves.

Carver's screw A stout screw with a large butterfly nut. In use, the screw is turned into the base of the wood to be carved, passed through a hole in the work bench and then secured with the butterfly nut.

Calipers Look like two curved legs which are pivoted at the crutch. In use they are set to a distance and then used for measurement transference.

Chip knife A short bladed, skew edged knife used for working chip carved patterns.

Chisel A flat bladed, hand-held tool. In use it can be held in one hand and then pushed with the other, or held in one hand and banged with a mallet. There are endless different types – skew, spoon bit and fishtail to name but a few.

Clamps and cramps A screw device for securing wood to the bench or pulling together two pieces of wood – they are variously called clamps, cramps, G-cramps and holdfasts.

Compass and dividers Simple two-leg instruments rather like calipers, used to draw out circles and strike off arcs.

Coping saw A thin bladed saw used for cutting curves in small section wood – see also **bow saw**.

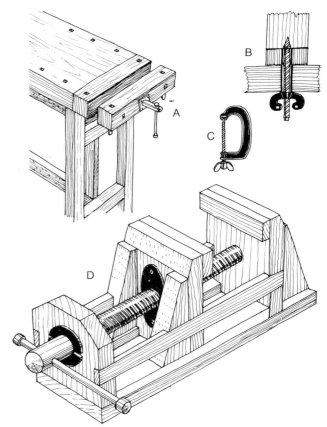

Holding equipment and workbench – **A**. Traditional woodworkers bench with stop or dog holes and end vice which hold the work. **B**. Bench screw – see how the screw is turned into the wood to be carved, is passed through a hole in the bench and held in place with the large wing nut **C**. A G-clamp **D**. Carvers chops and bench vices need to be well made, securely mounted and firm and strong enough for the job in hand.

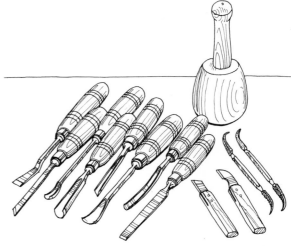

Woodcarving tools (reading from left to right) – a dog leg chisel, a skew chisel, a spoon bit gouge, a straight gouge, a V-tool, a broad spoon bit, a curved gouge, a straight chisel, a mallet, two chip knives and two rifflers.

Drawknife A two handled knife which is held in both hands and drawn along the wood towards the user. A good tool for cutting free shapes and curves.

Fishtail tool A straight chisel or gouge-section cutting tool with a fishtail shaped blade. A good tool for carving deep areas that are difficult to get at.

Gouge The most important of the wood carving tools, the gouge comes in over two thousand different shapes, types and sizes. A gouge is held in one hand and pushed with the other, or held in one hand and banged with a mallet. They differ from chisels in that the blade sections are shallow curved or deep V & U-shaped.

Holdfast Belong to the vice and clamp family in that they are used to hold wood secure.

Knife Wood carvers tend to adopt knives that come to hand. For example, I use a clasp knife, a penknife and a couple of old kitchen knives – if it suits my purpose I use it.

Mallet Traditional English mallets are round in section and usually made of Beech – a mallet is primarily a chisel or gouge-tapping tool.

Parting tool V-section tools belonging to the gouge family. Used to carve V-section cuts in incised work, relief outlining, etc.

Rasps and rifflers Files that are used for shaping wood. Rasps are generally used for large areas and rifflers for small, tricky nooks and corners.

Skew chisels A flat chisel with an angled cutting edge. Can be used for tight corners, chip carving and the like.

Slips and stones See section on tool sharpening on page 10.

Specialized tools Odd shaped chisels and gouges have been developed for specialized wood carving tasks. For example, a frame carver and boat builder would both have special tools like the fluteroni, maccaroni and dog-leg whose names usually describe the tool's usage, shape, or country of origin.

Spokeshave A plane-like tool with two handles used for working small curves.

Spoon bit tools Belonging to the gouge family, they are dished or spoon shaped at the cutting edge and used for scooping out bowls and tight concave curves.

Surform A registered name for a plane-like rasp. They come in many sizes and shapes and are used for roughing-out large pieces of wood.

Veiner A V-section gouge used for carving fine V-section cuts.

Vice Every carver needs a vice. They come in all shapes, sizes and types – small clamp vices, engineers' vices, all wood vices, carver's chops and so on. A vice needs to be strong, bench mounted and large enough for the job in hand.

List of timbers for carving

Apple A good, dark, dense-grained, hard wood. Comes in relatively small sizes – carves well and takes a good polish.

Ash A long-grained tough wood. Not really suitable for beginners.

Beech A heavy, pleasant to carve, inexpensive wood – has a yellowish sapwood and reddish heartwood.

Box (English) A beautiful butter-smooth pleasant smelling wood. It is hard and dense-grained and can't be bettered for small, special carvings.

Canary (American Whitewood) A yellowish soft wood, even grained and knot-free – easy to carve.

Cherry A close-grained, pleasant to work red/brown wood – carves well.

Chestnut Brown in colour – rather like Oak in that the grain is firm and compact. It carves well.

Holly A beautiful, close-grained ivory white wood – it carves well and takes fine details.

Lime Close-grained, knot free and comes in large sizes. The perfect wood for beginners in that it can be carved in almost any direction.

Mahogany There are a great many varieties of mahogany – Cuban, American, African etc. Generally speaking mahogany is pinkish brown, straight-grained and easy to carve and finish.

English Oak A strong heavy wood varying from being straight-grained, easy to work and beautiful to knotty, twisted, tool-breaking and horrible.

Pear Pinkish brown in colour, has a close grain, a satiny finish and cuts in any direction. A very nice wood to carve.

Pine There are many, many varieties and most of them are stringy, knotty and difficult to work. However, for a large bold carving, Pine can be used to good effect with the knots and grain shining out and enhancing the form.

Plum A beautiful warm brown wood, pleasant to carve with a fine grain and a hard smooth finish.

Rosewood A red to black wood. Not easy to carve and has a tendency to split – cuts cleanly and takes a good polish.

Sycamore A hard, light coloured wood, it has a firm compact grain and carves and finishes well.

Teak A tough, yellowish brown and close-grained wood, it takes detail, has an oily texture and finishes well.

Walnut Dark to light brown – a good wood for both small and large pieces. It carves well and takes a good polish.

Yew A fine wood, yellow/brown in colour. Although it cuts cleanly and takes a polish, it tends to be full of cracks and dead knots.

Checklist of timber faults

There is no such thing as a perfect piece of wood or a hundred per cent guarantee that such and such a piece of wood, although good to look at, is sound and workable throughout. The best we can do is look out for problem indicators and then try and spot the faults and flaws at an early stage.

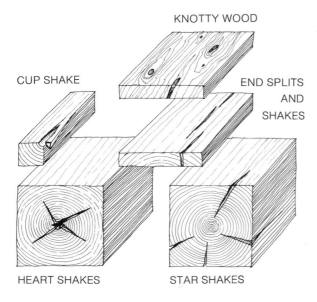

Faults in wood – cup shakes, heart shakes, knotty wood, end splits and star shakes. Wood is not a bland predictable material – in it's growing it sometimes develops faults and flaws. A good piece of carver's wood needs to be sound and workable throughout.

Decay If a piece of wood looks to be discoloured or shows signs of decomposition, sponginess, or pocket rot, it is likely to be unsuitable for carving – either cut away the bad wood, or better still look for another piece.

Checks If a board is cracked or split it is termed as having a 'check'. The defect might or might not be serious – my advice is to go for another piece of wood.

Shakes and splits Separations that occur throughout log lengths. For example, star shakes show as edge splits on log end-sections, and heart shakes show as open cavities. Maybe take the wood if it's a gift, but otherwise look for a better piece.

Knots These are termed as dead, hollow, live, loose, spiked and so on. They all tend to be difficult to carve, so if possible avoid them.

Blemishes Wood sometimes changes colour after it has been cut and looks to be stained. It is also easily stained by, say, rusty iron, grease or oil – if possible avoid stains.

Note: There are a great many other faults to be on the lookout for – foreign bodies within the wood; hidden cavities; cup shakes; unwanted waney bark wood; unexpected grain twists that relate to poor growth patterns, and so on. My advice is always double check your wood before you start carving, and if you have any doubt as to its quality, put it aside and look for another piece.

Glossary of technical terms

Blocking in Meaning to draw the lines of the design on the wood and establish the large important patterns and forms.

Bridge A slender area of supporting wood that is left in place throughout the carving, and cut away just before finishing.

Burnishing To take surface wood to a high finish by oiling, waxing or rubbing with a smooth tool.

Close-grained Wood that has narrow annual rings and consequently carves well.

Elevations In drawing, the view of an object. So a particular view might be described as end elevation or front elevation.

End grain Cross section grain at the end of a piece of timber.

Finishing The act of texturing, waxing or otherwise enhancing the appearance of a piece of carving.

First cuts Meaning the very first stage in the carving after the initial designing and drawing when sharp edge tools are used for the first time.

Found wood Taken to mean wood that can be collected on country walks, demolition timber or wood found when beach combing.

Green wood Wood that still contains sap; unseasoned wood that is worked before it has dried out.

Grid Meaning guide lines that are drawn onto plans or the surface of wood to be carved.

Ground Wood in and around the design, background wood that is lowered.

Grounding or wasting away The act of cutting away the wood in and around the main design so that it is at a lower level. A term used in relief carving to describe wood that is being cut away.

Hard wood Botanically speaking hard wood comes from broad leafed deciduous trees. It doesn't necessarily mean that a hardwood is harder to work than softwood but it's a term to describe a wood's general characteristics.

Housing joint A joint in which the end of one member is enclosed in the other without actually being a tenon.

Laminating The act of glueing, pegging or screwing together several pieces or layers of wood prior to carving.

Lowering Meaning to cut away background wood to leave the design in high relief. Can be termed grounding, or wasting.

Marking out Taken to mean the measuring and drawing on the wood prior to carving. When a piece of wood has been marked out it's ready to carve.

Maquette A working model, could be made of clay, card, soap, plastercine, wax or any other malleable substance.

Modelling The act of carving a design to completion – the carving process of shaping the wood.

Off-cuts Small pieces of wood that are left over after you have made your initial cuts. Pieces of spare wood that can be re-used.

Outlining Meaning to take a V-section tool and incise the drawn lines of the design.

Pencil press transferring The act of tracing a master design and then pressing through the tracing so that the lines of the design are transferred to the wood.

Piercing To fret, drill or cut wood so that only a tracery remains.

Plateau wood When the ground wood in and around the main design has been cut away and lowered, the relief design is sometimes termed plateau wood.

Pulling together Meaning to actually assemble various components, or to access the work in progress and critically rethink the design.

PVA Glue White wood working adhesive belonging to the family known as polyvinyl acetates.

Quick finish Meaning a finish that is made up of sharp, crisp cuts – a finish that is direct and not over sanded or fussed, sometimes called a swift finish.

Roughing-out Meaning to take a saw or chisel and roughly cut away the unwanted wood.

Seasoned wood Wood that is considered to have a low and workable moisture content. One man's seasoned wood could well be useless and overdry to another.

Setting in or setting-in. Meaning to separate the ground wood from the relief design. A design can be set in after the V-cut outlining and before or after the grounding depending on the character of the work. In practice, a design is set in by going around the design and making a vertical cut with a straight tool.

Setting out Meaning to transfer the design from the working drawing to the wood and establishing and organizing the grid and the cutting lines.

Short grain or short-grain. Taken to mean areas of wood where the structure of the grain is such that the wood is fragile and liable to split.

Stop-cuts An initial cut into which prior cuts are made – a stop-cut defines the length of subsequent cuts and acts as a safeguard.

Strap-work Relief carved ornamentation in the form of crossed or interlaced bands.

Tooled finish Meaning a finish that is textured with the marks left by the tools. It can be either a positive finish in that the surface is worked with a punch or it can be just a knife or gouge worked finish that is left unsanded.

Trenching The act of incising or cutting in pencil drawn lines with a V-section tool.

Undercutting Meaning deep relief work or nearly carving in the round – cuts that almost separate a motif from the main body of wood.

Waste Ground See wasting and ground.

Wasting See grounding.

Work-outs Meaning trial, dry run, experimental carvings prior to the real thing. Work-outs would use off-cuts and second quality wood.

Conversion table

inches	millimetres
$\frac{1}{32}$	0·8
$\frac{1}{16}$	1·6
$\frac{1}{8}$	3·2
$\frac{3}{16}$	4·8
$\frac{1}{4}$	6·4
$\frac{5}{16}$	7·9
$\frac{3}{8}$	9·5
$\frac{7}{16}$	11·1
$\frac{1}{2}$	12·7
$\frac{9}{16}$	14·3
$\frac{5}{8}$	15·9
$\frac{11}{16}$	17·5
$\frac{3}{4}$	19·1
$\frac{13}{16}$	20·6
$\frac{7}{8}$	22·2
$\frac{15}{16}$	23·8
1	25·4
2	50·8
3	76·2
4	101·4
5	127·0
6	152·4
7	177·5
8	203·2
9	228·6
10	254·0
11	279·5
12	304·8
18	457·2
24	609·6
36	914·4